Teaching Notes

on Piano Exam Pieces

2023 & 2024

Initial Grade to Grade 8

Timothy Barratt

Sharon Gould

Anthony Williams

ABRSM

First published in 2022 by ABRSM (Publishing) Ltd, a wholly owned subsidiary of ABRSM, 4 London Wall Place, London EC2Y 5AU, United Kingdom

© 2022 by The Associated Board of the Royal Schools of Music

ISBN 978 1 78601 493 1
AB 4057

A CIP catalogue for this book is available from The British Library.

Cover by Lloyd Winters, Kate Benjamin and Andy Potts, with thanks to Trinity School, Croydon
Printed in England by Caligraving Ltd, Thetford, Norfolk, on materials from sustainable sources

P15579

CONTENTS

FOREWORD

by ABRSM Chief Examiner, John Holmes

Choosing new pieces is always exciting – rather like setting out on a journey to somewhere you haven't been before. As a teacher, you are presented with an opportunity to match your students' skills and preferences to the right music for them, while also making use of your expertise to ensure the right level of challenge to encourage the development of technique and musicianship. This book is intended to help guide you in making good decisions, together with your student, about which pieces will work most successfully. It sets out to provide useful insights into each piece included in our books of *Piano Exam Pieces*, which we hope will support you and your students on your teaching and learning journeys. The expert contributors are all piano teachers with a wealth of examining experience. They are able to draw from their knowledge and understanding to provide valuable hints and tips, as well as helpful advice on how to develop the musical relationship that links composer, score and performer, and leads to successful performance.

In fact, the choice of piece is only the first in an almost infinite series of choices which becomes the learning journey I mentioned at the beginning. Whether it's Martinů, Mendelssohn or Milne, Price, Pescetti or Peterson, a whole range of decisions – conscious and subconscious – will need to be made in order for the developing pianist to arrive at their destination; in this case, the exam performance – be this live in the exam room or via an uploaded video. Tempo, touch, fingering, pedalling, phrasing ... the list of choices goes on, so perhaps it would be helpful here to talk about how the decision-making process might be approached.

It is crucial to say that there is no 'ABRSM way' of playing any of our listed piano exam pieces, although of course there *is* an 'ABRSM way' of assessing how they are performed. This is by considering the overall musical outcome – in effect, the cumulative result of all the various musical and technical decisions that will have been made in preparing the performance. For example, ABRSM examiners don't assess fingering, but we do comment on and evaluate its effects, such as evenness of tone or regularity of delivery, which are often partly the result of fingering choices. Examiners are listening and looking for the degree of skill a candidate shows in controlling elements of pitch, time, tone, shape and performance, which develop gradually during their learning and practice prior to the exam. It is these ingredients of music-making that form the basis of our marking criteria, which are used by examiners in all ABRSM Practical and Performance Grade exams.

Between them, the ABRSM scores, recordings and *Teaching Notes* are intended to open a variety of doorways to interpretation. There may well be differences between what the scores imply, what the recordings present and what these *Teaching Notes* recommend – but, in reality, they do not so much contradict as complement each other. We would like to encourage you to inspire your students to play with creativity and individuality, leading them to achieve successful performances that suit and reflect their particular skills, strengths and enthusiasms.

That's the excitement of every musical journey – there will always be a variety of routes to a successful musical performance, and our examiners do not mark candidates according to any particular one; instead they judge the combined effectiveness of the various musical decisions you and your student have made, taken as a whole. In the context of our digital exams, there is also the overall musical journey and sequence of the programme itself to consider, as well as thinking about each piece as an individual item. This means that every candidate can play to their strengths, not only in their particular choice of pieces but also in the way that they interpret them. For example, there is a range of tempos – a 'bandwidth' of speeds – at which any given piece can successfully be played. For some pieces this will be wider than for others, but even where a metronome mark is given, there is usually room for some flexibility of approach. The examiner will not be marking the chosen speed absolutely or in isolation, but rather in conjunction with other elements of performance, such as note accuracy and rhythmic character. The right tempo choice for each student is best determined as part of a comfortable balance with other elements, so that one aspect is not sacrificed to another – precision sacrificed to speed, for example.

Other decisions to be made include phrasing, ornament realisation, whether to add dynamics, play straight or swing quavers, and how much to use the pedal. The examiner will be assessing the overall musical outcome, rather than the strict observance of any printed pedal indications, which means that these may be adapted or omitted to suit the needs of the individual. However, it is important to bear in mind the strengths of your student so, for example, pieces whose full musical effect is heavily reliant on pedalling (whether marked in the music or not) might be best avoided if appropriate pedalling cannot be managed.

It is worth reiterating that using the ABRSM marking criteria (which can be found online), examiners will assess the overall musical outcome: the musical effectiveness of the piano playing within the exam context. The best results will arise from a well-judged match between each individual candidate's musical and piano skills and the particular demands of the chosen piece.

The pieces are grouped together by the characteristics of the music, making it clear what to expect from the pieces in each of the syllabus lists. List A pieces are generally faster moving and require technical agility, List B pieces are more lyrical and invite expressive playing, while List C pieces reflect a wide variety of musical traditions, styles and characters. At Initial Grade to Grade 3, duets are also an option (although they are not included in the books of *Piano Exam Pieces*), offering further choice and a different opportunity to build confidence at the early stages.

In face-to-face exams, candidates can choose the order in which they play their pieces (though if a duet has been chosen, it is preferable if it is played at the beginning), and whether to start the exam with these or another section – scales, for example. Of course, in digital exams the sequence and pacing of the recorded performance is entirely in the hands of the candidate. Once again, there is no single right way; as with so much of the musical learning journey leading to performance, the exam itself starts with a decision!

We do hope that you will feel excited and inspired by the wonderful range of musical possibilities open to you and your students within the 2023 & 2024 ABRSM Piano syllabus. Spanning nearly 400 years of composition, whether it's Chaminade or Chopin, there is truly something for everyone to discover and enjoy.

ABOUT THE AUTHORS

All of the authors have a wealth of teaching and examining experience, which covers a wide variety of musical styles. Each author has contributed to a mixture of grades and lists. The initials shown above each teaching note can be used to identify its author.

TIMOTHY BARRATT ARAM GRSM LRAM ARCM LMusTCL

Tim studied on a scholarship at the Royal Academy of Music and in Paris with Vlado Perlemuter. As a solo pianist, accompanist and chamber music player, he has performed extensively throughout the UK and abroad. He has considerable experience of teaching at all levels, as Head of Keyboard at Dulwich College from 1992–2016, and as a lecturer and vocal coach at the RAM and Trinity College of Music. He regularly directs courses for performers and teachers and is an ABRSM examiner and a member of the examiner training and review team.

SHARON GOULD MA ARCM

Sharon read music at Cambridge University and has performed extensively as a harpsichord soloist and Baroque orchestral director in the UK and internationally. As a pianist, she performs in a piano duo, as an accompanist and as a chamber musician. She has taught at the Royal College of Music Junior Department, Chetham's School of Music and the Royal Northern College of Music; her former students include several international award winners. She is a soprano in the Salisbury Cathedral Chamber Choir and sings in the six-voice ensemble 'Skylarks'. Sharon is an ABRSM examiner and a member of the examiner training and review team.

ANTHONY WILLIAMS MMus Dip.RAM GRSM ARAM

Anthony has an active performing, teaching and adjudicating career in the UK and abroad and is currently Head of Keyboard and Instrumental Music at Radley College, Oxfordshire, and Chairman of EPTA Europe. As a piano specialist he regularly presents teacher support lecture-recitals and is an examiner (jazz and classical) and a member of the examiner training and review team for ABRSM. He is author of the highly acclaimed *Piano Teacher's Survival Guide*, the compiler of *Fingerprints* and the *Best of Grade* series for piano, and editor of *Simply Classics* (all published by Faber Music).

HOW TO USE THIS BOOK

In *Teaching Notes*, every note contains teaching ideas relating to three areas of learning: musical context, technical challenges, and performance and interpretation.

Syllabus list numbers and author initials are shown at the top of each piece, either side of the composer name and piece title, for example:

A:1 **F. X. Chwatal** Little Playmates

 MUSICAL CONTEXT

The first section explains where the piece fits within the world of music and introduces the distinctive features of the piece. Genre, period, structure and style may be mentioned here, as well as information about the composer. You might also find suggestions of music to listen to, which will help your student gain familiarity with the musical context.

✋ TECHNICAL CHALLENGES

In this section the trickiest corners of the piece are identified and suggestions to help tackle them are provided. Alternative ornament realisations and fingering may appear here, as well as practice ideas to help with agility and coordination.

🎨 PERFORMANCE AND INTERPRETATION

This section focuses on communicating the music with style and personality. These elements can help turn an accurate performance into one with real artistic value.

General advice about interpreting the score, hand stretch, pedalling and repeats can be found in the relevant Piano syllabus, under 'Practical Grades: requirements and information' and 'Performance Grades: requirements and information' respectively.

INITIAL GRADE

A:1 **F. X. Chwatal** Little Playmates

🧩 The playmates of the title seem to be involved in lively discussion – maybe about the character of C major scales, as this cheerful little piece relies almost entirely on them.

✋ The main technical challenges will be balance and shape. It is never too early to nurture an independence of hands and the control to project a LH melody with character and shape above RH chords (and vice versa, of course). In bars 5 and 6, for instance, a gently placed RH chord starting from the surface of the key into the key bed will provide a soft harmony, while using some arm weight behind a fairly strong finger action in the LH will allow it to come to the fore. To help shape the phrase and convey the humour and charm, encourage your student to think of the LH as a gesture, falling into and across the first notes then lightening and lifting for the detached crotchets, while always keeping the articulation clear and tone focused to convey the marcato.

🎨 Bold dynamic contrasts will enhance the interest of the games and conversations, as will communicating the 'question and answer' nature of the piece. A rise and fall within each dynamic to shade the melody is crucial to its sense of fun and motion. The tempo doesn't need to be too fast; your student should focus instead on the musical interest, and perhaps even include a little rallentando at the end as the exhausted playmates run out of energy.

A:2 **Trad.** What shall we do with the drunken sailor?

🧩 Traditional songs have been passed down from generation to generation and more recently written down and recorded. It should go without saying that this tune will therefore be known by all our students, but sadly this is not so certain nowadays. Introduce them to the words, but also sing along with them; a confident communication of the story is crucial to encourage a vivid interpretation.

✋ The main challenge will lie in controlling and clearly articulating the repeated notes. The marked fingering will work, but even at this early stage I would be inclined to extol the benefits of a change of finger for the more coordinated pupils. In the opening RH figures, I would suggest 3-2-1-2 (and 2-1-5 in bar 4). In bars 5–6, try 1-3-2-1-3-2-1 and so on. This might seem fussy, but it always lends itself to greater evenness and control, and beds in a technique that will be crucial in later repertoire.

The dynamic contrasts will bring the song to life, but dynamic shaping of the phrases will add even more. This is where the words come in: match the rise and fall both towards and away from 'drunken' and 'Early', but then perhaps put an emphasis on 'What' in another phrase. Your student could save a special *p* for bar 17, so the crescendo can build dramatically to the *rit.*, keeping a confident *f* to the final (surprising) major chord.

A:3 **Heinrich Wohlfahrt** Patterns (AW)

The melodic patterns of the title are obvious, though the name does not do full justice to this elegant little piece, which feels part dance and part merry-go-round in its lilting three in a bar.

Balance between the hands and a delicate and expressive shaping of the melody are essential, especially in the opening bars. Slightly over-holding the LH bass notes (the Cs) with a subtle circular movement of the wrist will allow more harmonic support and help to lighten the end of each broken triad. A similar gesture across the RH quavers will also enhance the shape. In bars 9–10, a more mazurka-like stamp of the foot can be conveyed by a lift on the detached crotchet and relaxed fall back to the key bed with a giving wrist to soften the edge. Keep the quavers legato, perhaps practising a deliberate overlap of the notes at first to help the listening awareness and coordination.

Musically, the performance needs to convey a cheerful smile and buoyancy. Encourage your student to think of the dynamics as contextual, always shaping the phrases and never playing uniformly *f* or *p*. In bar 4, treat the staccato crotchets as just a gentle rise onto the dancers' toes – not too short and with a decrescendo through the bar. Students might consider the same in the LH of bars 11 and 12. The chosen tempo should allow good control throughout but, even more importantly, communicate the music's grace and charm.

B:1 **Ruth Schonthal** A Waltz that's a Little Melancholy (TB)

The descriptive title perfectly captures the thoughtful mood of this minor-key dance, with its gentle one-in-a-bar lilt. The texture allows the LH to take centre stage, while the RH provides much of the gentle dance-like flow. Singing the melody along with your student may help them to develop an all-important sense of phrasing.

Firm fingers, feeling to the base of the key, will allow the melody to sing, and a rounded hand position will enable control of the RH chords. Rests provide space to prepare RH moves, while slightly shortening the final note of each LH phrase will ensure a confident flow. The move in both hands at bar 13 needs particular care, and full value should be given to the dotted minim in bar 9.

🎨 Balance between melody and accompaniment is the principal musical challenge here. Interactive clapping, with your student, of the melody and quieter RH crotchets would encourage good listening, and practising silently shadowing the RH chords while projecting the melody might offer a practical solution. A shapely LH tone, well tapered at phrase ends, will capture the lyrical character. Your student could consider adding a gradual diminuendo as the melody descends towards bar 12, followed by a firmer restart in the following bar; a slightly earlier start to the final *rit.* might be preferred.

B:2 Fanny Waterman & Marion Harewood ⓉB
Swans and Ducks

🧩 This descriptive piece conjures up a scene of swans proudly and effortlessly gliding over a calm lake while neighbouring ducks move busily to and fro. Hand positions remain stationary, except for one LH move in the penultimate bar, leaving room for your student to concentrate on the important task of creating a legato LH line accompanied by quieter staccato chords.

✋ Isolating the LH line and listening for perfect joins between the notes, with no overlap of sounds, would be a good starting point. Firm fingers, supported by a supple wrist, will enable each note to sustain the slow-moving phrases, while gently releasing phrase ends will allow the melody to breathe. You may need to address with your student the coordination challenge of simultaneously producing legato and staccato. Initially practising away from the keyboard might help to establish the movements, starting, if necessary, by holding one LH finger while releasing one RH chord.

🎨 The relative size of swans and ducks is reflected in the contrasting dynamic levels between the hands. Close contact with the keys is needed to control the quietly pecking chords, uniformly short and evenly spaced, as the bass line sings proudly and confidently. In bars 5–8, well-graded hairpins mirror the shape of the melody, while the quietest moment is reserved for the ending.

B:3 Naomi Yandell Secret Footpath ⓉB

🧩 Imagine a stroll through a forest, quiet and perhaps slightly eerie. The path is a little meandering and you are not quite sure of the destination until the reassuring major chord is reached in the final bar. The unhurried footsteps are regular for the most part, yet with a few rests giving space to enjoy the surroundings. The short melodic phrases in this piece highlight the sense of mystery and uncertainty, while gentle, well-controlled textures help to create that all-important sense of secrecy.

✋ Holding both notes of the repeated LH shapes is one challenge to be addressed at the learning stage. Good key control here will provide a gentle harmonic framework, without any unwanted accents on the second-beat notes. Lifting both notes before the end of the bar, perhaps on the fourth beat, will ensure clarity on the repeated semibreves while maintaining the rhythmic flow. Care will be needed to place the fourth beat accurately in bars 4, 8 and 12, and rests (in bars 8 and 11) provide space to move seamlessly between the two RH positions.

 The *mf* at bar 9, which mirrors the slightly higher pitch at this point, gives variety and shape to the predominantly quiet dynamic level. The RH contours can be highlighted by a gentle rise and fall in the melodic fragments, and a well-judged final diminuendo, supported by a gradual slackening of pace, will bring this idyllic amble to a peaceful close.

[C:1] **Peter Gritton** Haunted House (SG)

Listening to *The Sorcerer's Apprentice* by Dukas would provide an excellent introduction to scary storytelling in music – even its opening bars conjure up suitably apprehensive feelings to inspire the *misterioso* mood of *Haunted House*. For further listening, 'Secrets of the Castle' from John Williams's soundtrack for *Harry Potter and the Prisoner of Azkaban* captures similar feelings of dread and anticipation.

Keeping a steady pulse at an appropriately slow tempo may prove challenging for your student, with both staccato notes and quavers liable to a hint of unwanted hurrying. Rhythmic clapping games that mimic the patterns in each two-bar phrase should help to avoid this if introduced in the note-learning stage. If your student is finding it difficult to play legato in one hand and detached in the other (which is required in several bars), isolating these bars for focused and repeated practice will encourage the necessary independence of hands.

The silences and staccatos in the music help to create the haunted atmosphere. Conviction in giving these their full due, along with careful attention to the different levels of quiet dynamics and rise and fall within the phrases, will allow the performance to communicate a ghostly presence that is felt rather than seen.

[C:2] **Kerstin Strecke** The Waltz of the Toads

Students who live near water may be familiar with toads. If not, a colourful photo should give them a memorable image for imagining this dance. The music uses a clever choice of sounds to describe the clumsy movement of toads, although the semitones that create the effect require unusual technical precision and definitely not clumsiness!

Because of the combination of white and black notes, a slight sideways, inwards turn of the wrist for sharpened notes may be needed to ensure that both notes sound simultaneously. A relaxed hand and thumb are desirable, nevertheless. When playing hands together, students should pay attention to the precise length of the LH minims, and it is important not to hurry the minim or the rest in bar 8.

In communicating the waltz feel, the LH melody (bars 1–4 and 9–12) would benefit from a slight lightening of the second- and third-beat crotchets, to increase the sense of arrival at the following bar. Choosing a little variety of dynamics, beyond the single *mf* marking in the score, would give your student a sense of ownership of this music and enhance their ability to play with enjoyment. A very grand *rit.* for the closing bars would add a final touch of polish to the playing.

⌞C:3⌝ **Diane Hidy** Jinx

A jinx is a curse or spell, and the sharp and flat notes definitely have an evil feel about them. In the early stages, your student might enjoy the experiment of replacing the 'cursed' notes with white-note alternatives, so that the effect of the actual printed notes is more meaningful to them.

The combination of frequent position changes and detailed dynamic and articulation instructions will present quite a challenge in terms of keeping a steady pulse. In the early stages of learning, a helpful approach is to break the piece down into small units: repeat bar 1 to the first note of bar 3 until all elements are safe, then follow the same process for bars 3–5 and so on. There is much repetition of material, so work on bars 1–14 will cover most of the piece. To land the RH crossovers accurately (bars 12 and 28), the journey over the LH should be made smoothly, during the four quavers of the preceding bar. Avoiding a last-minute dash will allow control of both tone and timing.

To create a storyline for inspiring the performance, your student could think about why the first six bars climb up in steps, getting gradually louder and then much slower before pausing. What is going on? Why do the hands cross over in bars 12–14? Of course, there is no one correct answer, but imagining a scenario will help to keep position changes on track and give a freshness to the communication.

GRADE 1

A:1 | **Anton Diabelli** Allegretto in C (TB)

Generations of students have been attracted to this graceful little piece, with its regular phrase structure and clear-cut texture. A combination of detached and slurred notes gives poise to the measured rhythms, while a gradual increase in dynamic level at each eight-bar section creates a sense of structure. The Alberti-bass figures in bars 17–21 are likely to present the main challenge for your student, thereby determining the most appropriate overall tempo.

While hand positions remain largely stationary, the few jumps will need careful practice. Rests at the end of each section give space to change position in both hands, while shortening the LH minim in bar 6, using the notes F-E as an anchor, will prevent any hiatus at the bar-line. A rounded hand position will ensure that all chord notes sound cleanly. Independence of hands is needed to coordinate the RH repeated notes with the LH quavers (bars 17–21), especially when changing fingers.

Each eight-bar section consists of two short phrases followed by a longer one. Shapely two-note slurs, with the second note lightly detached, feature throughout and enhance the music's graceful character. The LH plays a supporting role and will need careful balancing, while a well-controlled *p* at the start gives room for exploring the suggested terraced dynamics. Occasional checking with the metronome will ensure that a consistent pulse is maintained when the LH switches to quavers in the final section.

A:2 | **Marjorie Helyer** Dragonflies (TB)

Visualise sitting by a pond on a warm summer's day, watching the graceful undulating movements of these insects as they skim the water. A flowing yet unhurried tempo, with the quaver figures rising and falling effortlessly, will help to capture this idyllic scene. Although some RH quaver patterns move outside a familiar five-finger position, the composer provides sufficient space to prepare each group in advance.

The almost exact repeat of the opening eight bars at the end is a bonus at the note-learning stage. Evenness of tone and clear rhythmic pacing, with full value given to the dotted minims at the end of each section and a well-judged final *rit.*, are key ingredients for a convincing performance. Imagining the continuous quaver figures played by one hand may help your student to achieve a smooth, seamless transfer as the patterns switch between the thumbs, while a flexible wrist will enable the hand to float gently off the last note of each short slur. Close contact with the keys will enable good control of the figuration, while avoiding accents on each beat will convey that all-important one-in-a-bar feel.

Thinking in four-bar units will provide a sense of flow to each section. Subtly graded hairpins and a crescendo give direction to the middle section as the tonality shifts briefly to C major, with the f in bar 16 best understood in proportion to the overall tonal range. Elsewhere, the dynamic level does not rise above p, with the gentlest point reserved for the ending.

A:3 **Alexander Reinagle** Minuet in C   (TB)

The minuet is a familiar dance form that often appears in exam syllabuses, so it is refreshing to encounter one by a little-known composer, born in the same year as Mozart. Imagining the graceful gestures of elegantly dressed dancers in a sumptuous eighteenth-century palace might help your student to engage with a style that may feel remote from present-day experience.

A flowing tempo, unhurried and evenly paced, will help students to capture the graceful mood. Changes of hand position may need isolating, especially at bar 5, while care will be needed to maintain a consistent pulse when the quavers switch to the LH at this point. The common error of adding an extra beat at the double bar-line midway should be avoided. Clean release of each finger will give definition to the RH quavers, while the LH figuration in bars 5–6 (and 13–14) can be facilitated by a slight rocking movement, keeping the thumb close to the key.

Conveying the natural rise and fall of each four-bar phrase within its own dynamic level is the key to an expressive performance. Clear articulation of the mixture of slurred and detached notes will provide interest to the melodic line, while lighter second and third beats will give clarity to the dance rhythms.

B:1 **Andrew Eales** Fresh Air   (SG)

The weightless atmosphere described by the composer in the footnote to the score might be successfully explored by listening to 'Venus' from Holst's *The Planets*. Similarly lacking low and fast notes, this lovely orchestral piece would make a helpful starting point for discovering the gentle but singing touch needed to convey the sensation of gazing into clear skies.

As the pedal is marked in the closing bars, encourage your student to form the habit of sitting forwards on the stool before the start of the piece (unless a pedal extender is used), to avoid any last-minute shuffling and disturbance in flow. This will enable the heel to stay firmly connected to the floor when the pedal is in use. In the RH of bars 13–14, careful counting of both the minim and the crotchet rest should be followed by a smooth position-shift, with no bump on the thumb note. Releasing the LH chords a fraction before the bar-lines will enable the melody to remain legato where marked.

A warm, melodic sound and softer balance for the accompanying notes will support effective communication of the music's character. To preserve the required weightlessness, the descending intervals (e.g. in bars 5–7, RH, and bars 17–18, LH) can be shaded away as they fall. Adding a very slight delay before the final high G, while also giving it firm weight, will allow it to resonate convincingly.

B:2 Florence B. Price A Morning Sunbeam (SG)

Composers throughout history have been inspired by thoughts about daybreak. To get a feel for this little piano piece, your student could listen to the opening of Haydn's Symphony No. 6, 'Le matin', which illustrates early-morning calm enlivened by the light of the rising sun, or to Nielsen's 'Helios' Overture – an especially apt choice, as its morning sunbeams are similarly first depicted in pairs of rising long notes. For helpful visual images, students could turn to Van Gogh, Monet or Turner, among many others.

Few keyboard shifts are required to play this gentle piece, which mostly preserves a natural five-finger hand position. The shifts at bars 17, 33 and in the last line need to be accomplished without rushing or hesitancy, so can be given extra practice for the sake of security. Other technical challenges are balancing the slow-moving RH melody against the more active LH broken chords, along with controlling the tone as parts of the melody move from one hand to the other. Maintaining a feeling of firm downward pressure in the fingertips of the melodic hand, with a lighter, floaty finger-action for the broken chords, should help with balance here.

For a polished performance, observing the longer phrasing in the middle section will provide musical interest. The crescendo in bars 31–2 may be thought of as leading into the main theme's return with an enthusiastic sense of expectation. The last line offers a restful conclusion; neat hand-crossing in bars 47–50 will help to avoid tonal bumps in the lead-up to the more resonant timbre of the fully risen sun in the closing four bars.

B:3 Michael Head The Quiet Wood (SG)

There is little in this music to suggest any specific images of the scenery. This presents a marvellous opportunity for your student to imagine the surroundings for themselves, especially in the way that some phrases are quite short and others much longer. Perhaps the short phrases tell of a flower beside a log, while the long ones describe the view along a tree-lined path, or a woodpecker flying across a sunny glade.

There are quite a few changes of position (e.g. between bars 2 and 3), and these need to be achieved without a tonal bump on the preceding note. There is time to move in a controlled way, however, because an unhurried feel between phrases will add to the musicality of the playing. Creating the required singing tone may need some experimentation: students may find it helpful to think of playing right down to the key bed, with a little pressure from the knuckles, rather than just tickling the tops of the keys.

As the melody passes from one hand to the other (in bars 9–10 and bar 20), the volume should be well matched. In bar 15, the repeated RH E needs a smooth change from finger 4 to finger 5. The performance will benefit from musical shape in the phrasing – for example, the addition of a small crescendo on the rising crotchets in bars 3 and 9.

[C:1] **Shruthi Rajasekar** Virginia Hall

This enticing piece cleverly conveys the American influence of both the composer and the spy it is named after. There are bold hints of blues in the melodic line, and the spy's connections to the Allied Forces are maybe present in the persistent rhythmic RH accompaniment, reminiscent of Morse code.

The RH figurations need subtle control of dynamics, rhythm and articulation, easily achieved by a gentle, relaxed bounce from the wrist onto rounded, supported fingers. It doesn't need much energy from the fingers themselves, or there is a risk the tone will become initially rather too forthright and intrusive. Your student should make sure the LH tune projects warmly, using plenty of arm weight; a genuinely legato tonal overlap between notes will give it more of a vocal, gospel-like sense of line.

The performance will rely on its musical narrative to draw the audience in, the nervous staccato and suspicious dynamic hairpins adding to the subversive character, and the bold crescendo and dynamic contrast in bars 10–12 conveying the dramatic climax. Your student could aim for an almost ruthless *ff* in bar 12 and then sustaining a bold *f* through to bar 17 before allowing the dynamic to fall. No ritardando is marked at the end, nor is one needed; simply do what is notated with the softest of final motifs as the spy disappears back into the shadows.

[C:2] **Martha Mier** Sneaky Business

This aptly titled and characterful piece from the composer's *Jazz, Rags & Blues* series is full of subterfuge and hiding in shadows in its articulation and dynamics.

The syncopated rhythm may need some preliminary work. Clapping it as a duet against the pulse will help, thinking of the offbeat chord as a jokey interruption. Then perhaps isolate the RH from bars 25 to the end, where the harmonies change quickly and the syncopation is most prevalent. Here, your student could practise the rhythm using just the top notes at first but with the marked fingering, then add the lower notes, allowing the hand to drop into the key for the start of each bar and rise for the staccato crotchets to give it some shape. In the LH, an even, light and controlled staccato is needed in the opening bars and in similar places. I would achieve this from the surface of the key with just a little energy, weight and bounce through the fingertips to the key bed.

Throughout, students could think of tiptoeing from shadow to shadow, the hairpins a temporary fear of being discovered; holding the notes of the chords as marked in bars 3–4 and so on will help to build up the tension. The final bars are perhaps where the torch is turned on and the shady character revealed. Students can make lots of the *f* here and use the pedal to enhance the final chord, lifting with the final bottom A. Gotcha!

C:3 **Caroline Tyler** Little Whale Explores the Calm Sea

With its atmospheric pedal, pictorial title and imaginative tonal colours, this intoxicating piece has many of the ingredients of a Debussy prelude. *La cathédrale engloutie*, with its underwater sound-world and story, would be inspiring listening before learning this piece.

The pedal is held through the first 20 bars as an effect, but resonance soon builds up so encourage astute listening and the lightest of touches to enable subtle adjustments to the balance of sound. A gentle use of weight and a flatter-finger caressing of the key surface will draw out the softest mellow tone. The brighter reflections of the sunlight in bars 3–6 might use a little more of the ends of the fingers to give the required intensity. In bar 24, your student should play the chord without pedal and avoid releasing it until the pedal is down. Conversely, the chord in bar 21 needs to be held, even though the pedal lifts.

This is a musical picture, so the dynamic hairpins and contrasts are important – particularly the *f* in bar 17, which depicts the whale and deep water. Keeping a broad and unhurried pulse is crucial, so students could experiment with counting the three beats in a bar as thousands ('one thousand, two thousand,' etc.) across each six-bar phrase to avoid any rushing or sense of urgency. A little slowing of the pulse across the final three bars wouldn't be amiss, with a most gentle, long-held final chord and slow lift of the pedal as twilight falls.

GRADE 2

A:1 **Ludwig van Beethoven** Écossaise in G (SG)

To introduce the style of this jolly tune, originally written for wind band, you might listen with your student to some online recordings of any Beethoven écossaises or marches for wind band, with their cheerful contributions from drums and triangle. Your student might also enjoy listening to Mozart's Rondo 'Alla Turca' – another, slightly earlier, piece that recreates the sounds of an outdoor band on the piano keyboard.

Good foundations for reliable note-placement can be laid by practising the LH alone in bars 1–7, with each bar played as a solid chord. For further security, your student could start at the last LH quaver of each bar (having first checked its fingering), then practise the following two quavers, concentrating on landing all three quavers accurately. The athletic LH jumps of bars 9–12 may entail a few glances down to the keyboard, but fortunately the RH is straightforward at this point.

The music's sunny nature comes from the RH melody, which will benefit from clear contrasts of touch between p and f dynamic levels. The characterful semitone step to A♯ in the RH of bar 4 needs conviction; a feeling of growing in volume here should provide impact. Playing bars 11–12 slightly louder or softer than bars 9–10 could add interest to the performance, as could extra dynamic variety in shaping the last line, with confidently resolute accents in bars 13–14.

A:2 **J. L. Dussek** Gavotte in F (SG)

Gavottes were a traditional part of the eighteenth-century dance suite, first in France and, famously, in the suites and partitas by J. S. Bach. Most frequently starting on the third beat of a four-beat bar, the first point of rhythmic emphasis was therefore after the first bar-line. With this in mind for Dussek's Gavotte, unusually laid out by the composer with bar-lines after every second beat, the rhythmic scheme will develop an elegant flow if the first bar is thought of as leading to the second, and the third to the fourth, and so on.

Although the texture may initially appear to be melody and accompaniment, in most phrases the LH line takes on a characterful duetting role. In bars 17–21, however, the LH thumb is in accompanying mode, with its repeated middle Cs. Separate technical practice to strengthen the fingers playing the LH melody here, with the middle C sustained above, will be helpful in keeping the thumb notes inconspicuous. A thumb kept fairly close to the key surface should then be able to repeat with reliable gentleness.

In creating a stylish performance, the phrasing can be shaped to lead forwards by becoming slightly louder as quavers rise and softer as they descend. Pairs of crotchets (apart from slurred ones) could be lightly detached, to convey a sense of dance. This will recreate the subtle gracefulness of the courtly gavotte and give a cheerful conversational feel to the crotchets passing from one hand to the other.

[A:3] **Agnieszka Lasko** Tarantella (SG)

This Tarantella comes from a beautifully illustrated book of pieces in which the composer encourages the player to create their own stories for the music. Some of the titles immediately suggest activities, moods or scenes for the story creation to start from. 'Tarantella' leaves a blank canvas, although the rapid tempo and energetic character of the wild dance on which it is based might recall an enjoyment of gymnastics or dancing, or excitable romping around.

The arpeggios in bars 9-10 and 13-14 may require extra practice, to ensure that they are smooth, reliable and played with the requested crescendo. Timing the links between one hand and the other will be more successful when each hand is ready in position a little in advance of its moment to play. An occasional check that the three-note chords are well coordinated would be worthwhile, especially in bars 33-9, where the usual roles of the hands are reversed.

The music's vitality will be best communicated if notes or chords at the mid-bar point are less robust than the downbeats. In the middle section (bars 9-24), extending this idea so that not all the downbeats are equally strong would help to drive the music forwards; bars 11, 15, 18, 20 and 22 might not contain a stress at all. The quiet finish, after so much excitement, is a witty touch, as if the gymnast/dancer/champion has simply run away.

[B:1] **Stephen Duro** Forget-me-not Waltz

Indulge in a little Johann Strauss II before introducing this piece. A few minutes listening to *The Blue Danube* will get the feet moving and body swaying, and be more informative about choice of tempo, light upbeats and melodic shape than any number of words.

There are two passages I would approach initially. Bars 9-12 feature a cheerful conversation between the hands. Your student could spend some time practising these bars with the RH *f* and the LH *p*, then vice versa, finally communicating the lovely interplay between the hands. The second passage is bars 21-4. Bar 22 has that wonderful 'going over a humpback bridge' feeling, the quaver rest suspending the dancers in mid-air for just a brief second before a bend of the knees returns them to the ground. Hands need to show the rest too, so can be suspended above the keys before returning to the pianistic dance floor.

 The melody needs lots of expressive shape and a confident, orchestral string-like tone, growing in dynamic through each of the first three phrases. The LH accompaniment needs plenty of light and shade, with gentle and quiet lifts on the second and third beats in bars 2, 4 and so on, and should be generally out of the way elsewhere. Make a feature of the *rit.* in bar 16, separating the end of the phrase from the upbeat quavers, and crescendo through bars 25–8 to allow for the subsequent diminuendo and *rall.*, the tired dancers returning home to bed.

B:2 **C. V. Stanford** Lullaby

Lullabies seem to have a universal musical language, the words of the first-known etched in clay around 2,000 BC. Their $\frac{6}{8}$ or three-in-a bar lilt is influenced by the rocking of a child in its mother's arms or a cradle, and the sleepy and comforting character needs no abrupt accents or strong articulation in performance. Therein lies the main technical challenge of this poetic and charming piece.

A good legato within phrases is de rigueur but will need some practice, particularly in the adjacent 3rds. I would isolate the LH of bar 3 and play the first 3rd then also the second, holding all four notes before releasing the first pair. Do the same with the RH 3rds in bar 10. In the LH of bars 7–8, release the bottom Bs but overlap the top notes to convey a legato accompaniment.

The gently rocking cradle is musically in evidence from the first bar. A soft drop into the keys for the first notes of the couplet phrase, followed by a gentle, quiet lift and the smallest silence at the bar-line, will shape the phrases like the breaths of a child. In bar 3, the rocking cradle continues in the LH with **pp** second beats, while the melody sings in expressively shaped phrases above. Bars 9–13 become just a little bolder, perhaps as the child stirs; students should show the crescendo in bar 12 but also, just as crucially, the gradual decrescendo from bar 17, perhaps with a rallentando just towards the end.

B:3 **Trad. Chinese** Kangding Love Song

 A musical world tour courtesy of a video or audio streaming site will reveal some truly wonderful and haunting traditional music in which the pentatonic scale is a prominent feature. The melody of this Chinese love song is no exception.

It would be worth visiting bar 10 to the end first. The coordination between the hands is more challenging here, and the rests crucial to the interplay between what could be two singers – a 'call and response' between the hands. Precise lifts of the hands are part of the music's character, so encourage slow, thoughtful practice, holding the tenuto crotchets and the minims for their full length (but not more) and characterfully shaping the phrases. At the start, the LH needs a warm carpet of harmony. Consider over-holding the notes, effectively thinking of the triad as always down at the key bed but lifting the fingers just enough to gently replay the notes. The thumb needs to be particularly controlled to avoid offbeat accents.

Encourage students to give the opening RH tune lots of expressive dynamic shaping, exploring the phrasing a little more literally than usual, as if conveying the articulation of the Chinese words. Keep the tempo at a gently flowing four in a bar, not two; there is no need for much rubato at all, just delicate shading throughout. A little breath at some bar-lines would be totally appropriate. Students should save room for the *pp* in bar 15 and convey a lovely, delicate *rit.* in the final bars.

C:1 David Blackwell Railroad Blues (TB)

This rail journey, with its laid-back swing rhythms and regular crotchet beat, is far removed from modern-day high-speed travel, yet there is nevertheless a sense that the destination will be reached with patience on the part of the traveller. The 12-bar-blues pattern, often a useful starting point for improvisation, provides a sense of structure, while a rock-steady tempo will set the mood for the long trip.

Establishing the LH chords that underpin the melodic line for much of the piece would be a good starting point. A curved hand position, slightly separating each crotchet, will ensure equally clean attack on both chord notes. Some preliminary work on the RH dotted figures, perhaps using a G major scale, would help your student to develop the all-important swing feel, if necessary subdividing each figure into three triplet quavers. An evenly spaced triplet in bar 3 can be ensured by initially removing the tie.

After establishing the ponderous character at the start, the LH immediately assumes an accompanying role. In the RH, releasing the final note of each bar on the fourth beat is a clean option for defining the different registers, and your student might like to explore a dynamic contrast between the phrases, in the manner of 'call and response'. Finger legato will sustain the chords in bars 12 and 24, while care will be needed to maintain the deliberate tempo throughout the louder second 'verse'.

C:2 Elissa Milne Mozzie (TB)

The restless energy of a mosquito is perfectly captured in the short jagged rhythms and repeated melodic patterns of this piece. The composer's detailed articulation and accentuation instructions help to bring the jazzy idiom to life, while clear-cut dynamic levels provide interest and variety.

A stable sense of pulse underpinning the syncopated rhythms is the most important requirement for a confident performance. Pinpointing exactly where the main beats occur is a good starting point for understanding the rhythm. Playing some interactive clapping games and inventing words to fit rhythmic figures are two fun methods for developing a rhythmic sense. Rests, which should be given full value, facilitate changes of hand position, and independent movement in the LH – releasing the semibreve chord early – is needed to avoid disturbing the melodic flow in bars 11–12.

Crisp LH articulation and alert rhythms capture the energetic character from the outset. Accents – some adorned with grace notes, played either with or slightly before the main note – highlight main beats, and a gentle *mp* at the start will give sufficient room for a dynamic contrast in bar 5. A momentary change of mood occurs at bar 9, with hairpins in bars 9–10 lending shape to both hands, before more frequent accents and shorter slurs lead to the *ff* climax in bar 13. The firmest attack is reserved for the four-note chords in bar 16, during which this irritating insect is perhaps eventually silenced!

C:3 Kristina Arakelyan Daydream   (TB)

This thoughtful piece is an ideal vehicle for exploring sensitivity and imagination in playing. Its slow-moving harmonic changes create a sense of spaciousness, while the gentle dynamic range, which never rises above *mf*, ensures that the dreamy atmosphere remains undisturbed. Control of tone is a chief requirement for a convincing performance, so testing the instrument's key and pedal response at the start of the exam would be wise.

Close contact with the keys is essential, especially at quieter levels, while slightly over-holding the triadic figures will serve to sustain the harmonies. Confident hand coordination will ensure fluency when moving off the tied notes from bar 9 onwards, and any rushing can be prevented by initially sub-dividing the dotted crotchets at bars 9 and 13 into quavers. Similarly, the rest in bar 21 needs careful pacing. Placing the foot over the pedal before the start of the piece will prevent a scramble later on.

Perfectly smooth, even quavers, with LH chords held for their full length, establish the mood at the opening. Stressing the LH notes in bars 8 and 25 will suggest moments of surprise in this idyll. Opportunities to highlight the imitation between the hands occur midway (from bar 9), and the end of each RH phrase can be punctuated by a slight separation. While the main climax occurs at bar 17, gentle rise and fall will breathe life into each phrase, before the music gradually fades away to a whisper.

GRADE 3

Anon. Minuet in G

It is a common belief that a lot of the short, easier Baroque and Classical dances written for the keyboard were used for teaching purposes, but it is also very likely that many were danced to. A quick visit to YouTube will reveal the graceful movements of a minuet and give a strong indication of the tempo and light upbeats that give this piece its charm.

In preparation, take your student straight to bars 21–4, as it is here that many performances will go rhythmically astray. Some clapping work from triplets to duplets will be invaluable. The leap from bar 18 to bar 19 is also a common hurdle. Some repetition of bar 18 to the first notes of bar 19, confidently finding the notes, will help.

Light RH crotchets at the ends of bars 2 and 4 should immediately convey the elegance of this dance. A relaxed drop into the first beat of these bars, lateral movement across to the second and a gentle lift on the third will give a dance-like gesture and decrescendo.

Dynamic shaping to the middle of each of the opening two-bar phrases, and a gentle, 'bend of the knees' emphasis on the first beats of bars 5 and 6 (and similar) followed by light second and third beats, will all give the music grace. Detach some crotchets, but a slight shortening is all that's needed. The dynamics are editorial, so your student should also consider their own. No ritardando is needed at the end of the first section, but a small holding back and placement of the final crotchets in the LH would be quite delightful.

Muzio Clementi Vivace

Witty and charming, this dance-like, chatty third movement of Clementi's popular Sonatina in C (Op. 36 No. 1) has bags of personality.

Good C major scales are essential. I would look with your student at the semiquaver runs first, making sure the fingering is decided and consistent and that fingers can control and, crucially, dynamically shape them, avoiding a first-note accent particularly when a run begins on an upbeat. A gentle and unobtrusive LH accompaniment will be essential to allow the melody plenty of dynamic space for characterful shaping. The LH broken chords should lighten as they go through the bar, perhaps with a slightly over-held bass note to support the harmony, and students should use the rests to travel to the next hand position for the loud, trumpet-like RH chords that herald the end.

There are numerous opportunities to convey the humour and playfulness of this music, including light, shorter second- and third-beat quavers; lots of dynamic rise and fall in the phrases; and some bold – perhaps surprising – dynamic contrasts. Bars 30–33 provide a wonderful opportunity to tease the listener with a subtle 'what's coming next?' rallentando to the semiquavers, then an accelerando back into the original tempo at bar 35. The performance doesn't want to be too fast; Vivace is simply 'lively' in Italian, so this should be conveyed in the musical detail, not just with the speed. The final chord could be placed after a fractional delay – almost a 'that's all folks!' gesture.

A:3   Mirosław Gąsieniec   Hansel and Gretel

This is a gem of a piece. It begins naively and simply in D major but then, to reflect the characters of Hansel and Gretel, changes personality, shifting abruptly to B flat major then back again. I suspect the lower melody is Hansel. If you don't know the story already, now's the time to start reading *Grimm's Fairy Tales*!

I would start by heading straight for bars 9–16; Hansel's song is the trickiest and needs to be confidently shaped and projected under a rather busy RH. Audiences will always want to listen to the higher notes, so a much softer RH is needed here than you might think. It may help to practise the RH in triads first, then – with a relaxed arm and holding each triad down – to lift each finger in turn just enough to replay the notes. This will give wonderful control for a soft accompaniment. The final two bars are also worth focusing on; some 'shadow jumping' (quick movements to jump and cover the next notes before playing) will be useful in the last bar.

To provide inspiration for shaping phrases and articulating quavers, encourage your student to think of the piece as a cheerful, carefree conversation between the two children, and to consider what they might be saying or singing. Some obvious dynamic contrast between the sections will also help with the characterisation. The tempo should be gently flowing but not too fast; the witch has clearly not yet made an appearance!

B:1   Nancy Litten   The Sad Ghost

The creepy title and character of this piece is likely to have popular attraction regardless of whether your student considers this ghost scary or friendly. The minor tonality and meandering lyrical melody, underpinned for much of the time by a regular LH rhythmic tread, creates a sense of mystery. Key elements in bringing this ghostly scene to life include reliable rhythmic poise, a sense of overall tonal shape and confidence over the whole keyboard.

A firm cantabile, perfectly smooth, will convey the phrasing, while careful listening is essential for gauging the long crescendos and diminuendos. A few coordination issues may need addressing, especially at the opening; careful counting, initially subdividing into quavers if necessary, will ensure that fluency and poise are maintained. Holding the fifth-finger bass notes from bar 7 for as long as possible before shifting to the new position will provide a firm harmonic foundation. The final six bars are perhaps best learnt by rote. Reliable LH fingering is vital here, and initially 'blocking' the RH 4ths will help to establish the repeated shapes.

An air of caution pervades the opening as the ghost seems to survey the scene, the quietest, shortest staccato notes in bars 3 and 6 suggesting wariness. Confidence grows through the cantabile phrases, which swirl upwards towards the climax at bar 20. However, the steep diminuendo that follows suggests that this assurance is short-lived. The sparse texture and ascent to the upper reaches of the keyboard from bar 25 allow this spirit to disappear without trace.

B:2   C. A. Loeschhorn   Study in F   (TB)

This beautiful and charming piece, with its undulating melodic line and gently flowing bass line, deserves a more imaginative title than Study in F! An atmosphere of calm contentment pervades the piece, with just a momentary suggestion of sadness as the tonality switches from major to minor at bar 9. Although a few LH patterns might catch out a less-confident student, the chief challenge lies in projecting the songlike character.

A good starting point for developing a rich cantabile line in the RH would be to do some slow practice on a five-finger pattern, using a gentle pressure from the arm through to the fingertips while keeping the wrist supple. Giving a slight prominence to the lower bass line, by slightly over-holding the fingers while keeping the repeated thumb notes light, will create a harmonic foundation for the main melody. Some changes of position may need particular care, especially in bars 6–7, and the semibreves (e.g. in bar 7) should be sustained for their full length.

Imagining the melodic line played by a string or wind instrument – or, better still, singing it – will help your student to sustain a legato line on the piano. The suggested *mf* indications in bars 13 and 20 represent high points within a gentle overall dynamic range, with natural inflections suggested by the hairpins. Definition will be given to the RH phrasing by lightly detaching the ends of slurs. Despite the chiefly supporting role of the LH, moments of special melodic interest – for example, the scale figure in bar 8 – are worthy of greater significance.

B:3   Yoshinao Nakada   The Song of Twilight   (TB)

The magical atmosphere of this jewel-like piece is likely to appeal to your student's imagination, and the chordal texture that hugs the melody for much of the time creates a timeless, almost hypnotic effect. A sensitively shaped RH melody and skilful balance between the hands will be key factors in an effect-ive performance.

If your student hasn't already explored legato pedalling, this piece would be a perfect vehicle for introducing it. A simple pedal exercise (e.g. a slow C major scale using the same finger) will help to establish the principle of releasing the pedal fully on, not before, each new sound. Isolating the LH will serve both to secure the transition between chords and to coordinate the pedal changes, which occur on each new harmony. Close contact with the keys is essential for creating a gentle, cushion-like texture above which the RH line can project unhindered.

Each short, one- or two-bar phrase offers scope for gentle inflection to reflect the semiquaver shapes, within a positive *p* dynamic that leaves room for the even quieter final section. The brief switch to the relative minor at bar 9 seems to suggest a different colour – perhaps bars 9–12 could be slightly louder – while leaving bar 12 without pedal will give clarity to the staccato crotchets. Use of the *una corda* pedal, the foot in position before use, will help to enhance the twilight atmosphere of the *pp* repeat.

C:1 Sonny Chua T-Rex Hungry

The engaging composer Sonny Chua captured the dinosaur's fierce person-ality memorably in this piece, which is almost entirely in the bass clef and fast. Chua had a keen rapport with young pianists and produced dozens of pieces for them, with catchy titles such as 'Bedtime Stomp', 'Byte Me', 'Headache Crawl' and 'Conquering Time and Space'. His important message to players of 'T-Rex Hungry' is quoted in the footnote.

Firm, even fingerwork will help your student to find the music's energy. A small rotation of the wrist, side to side, will support fluidity of movement in the many repeating legato patterns from the start. The writing contains much dissonance, including augmented 4th intervals (bar 11 onwards) and fre-quent chromaticism, so the aggressive mood is clear. The indication 'Tiptoeing' (for bars 13–14 and 17–18) would suggest a reduction in volume, but even here a crisp touch will be required to keep the rhythm exact.

Chua's message to the performer refers to attacking the accents and making the dynamic contrasts extreme. While this might be effective for the 'loudest snap' at the end, the risk of producing harsh sounds at the piano calls for consideration, and elsewhere a pungent resonance and plenty of tonal var-iety would produce a more entertaining performance. Technically, this can be achieved by maintaining flexibility in the hands and forearms, avoiding excessive rigidity of touch for accents and *sf* notes. There is no doubt about the composer's request for a fast tempo and strong pulse; the only danger here is of rushing as the excitement builds.

C:2 **William Gillock** The Spanish Guitar

The guitar forms part of most ensembles accompanying Spanish flamenco dancers. The dance has ancient origins but found its recognised style during the twentieth century. Traditional flamenco costumes are often featured in paintings. Leonid Afremov painted a series of flamenco-inspired pictures that can be viewed on the internet, notably *Passion of the Dance*. Its colourful vitality provides an excellent image to inspire characterful playing of this piece.

The many triplets each need to roll evenly into the following quaver, with no sense of jerkiness. These four-note groups, especially those in bars 3–4 and 7–8, might be isolated for focused practice, repeating until a smooth tone and rhythm have been gained. Still more demanding are the triplets in the penultimate bar, with their octave leaps, varied strong or weak position in the rhythmic scheme and decreasing volume. The *pp* LH 5ths (bars 9–18) require great precision over a long period; keeping fingertips close to the keys will help to avoid any tonal bumps and loss of pace.

Once this groundwork has been achieved, a lively tempo will help your student to find the flamenco style. It will also help to imagine a proud demeanour for the dance movements, rather than a gentle one, even in bars marked at quieter levels. Although the pace might ease up a little in the beat before a pause, elsewhere a strict pulse drives the dance forwards. Faithfulness to the composer's dynamic details can bring alive the colours and shapes of this fiery dance.

C:3 **Scott Joplin** The Entertainer

One reason for the popularity of ragtime music is its use of syncopation to play with our expectation of rhythm. *The Entertainer* is especially popular and uses syncopation in two ways: the normally weak second and fourth beats of the bar are stressed by double notes in the LH, and the RH quavers are frequently tied across a beat.

The few phrases that repeat material reduce the amount of music to learn, but care will be needed to avoid taking wrong turns when these phrases finish in different ways (compare bars 8 and 16, and bars 24 and 32). For students who prefer to read the music while playing, this may not pose a problem, although some preparatory work may be needed to ensure safe LH position changes; bars 12–13, 20–21 and 28–9 are particularly liable to errors in this respect. LH accuracy can be more easily watched by those playing mostly without reading the music, but the journey of the phrases will require good aural memory.

While most students will respond enthusiastically to the *giocoso* marking at the start, they may overlook the 'Not fast'. This is also important in locating the true spirit of the piece, however. For final polish, the two types of rhythmic detail described above – as well as the RH fourth-beat crotchets in bars 1, 2 and 7 – can be given a nudge of extra-firm tone, to project the syncopated style with character.

GRADE 4

A:1 **G. B. Pescetti** Presto · TB

The composer's delight in weaving a melodic line based purely on scale and arpeggio figures can be sensed throughout this energetic, joyful movement from the Sonata No. 6 in C minor. Confidence and stamina are needed to maintain fluency, but your student will doubtless enjoy the physicality of this RH workout, while also discovering the music's charm and elegance.

Clarity in RH fingerwork is the chief technical challenge here. A slightly detached touch, using the tips of the fingers, will give definition to the scalic figures that dominate much of the piece, whereas a smoother touch would highlight the harmonic progressions formed by the triadic patterns in bars 9–13 (and elsewhere). Anticipating the jumps between phrases by shortening the final crotchet would prevent any hesitation at the bar-lines, and your student may need to memorise the arpeggio descent in bars 68–72. The dotted figures in bar 52 should be converted into crotchet-quaver triplets, in line with standard stylistic practice. Placing the grace notes in bars 59 and 66 together with the main note will prevent any loss of fluency at the bar-line, while initially omitting the trills will help to maintain fluency at the cadences.

While the RH plays the dominant role throughout, the bass line serves to underline the harmonic structure while also providing impetus to the phrasing. Detached LH crotchets would be a stylish option for much of the movement, whereas phrasing the minims in two-bar units (e.g. in bars 9–12) will highlight the sequences. Clear-cut dynamic contrasts, as if played on different harpsichord manuals, would lend character to the echo effects suggested throughout, while the musical contours can be conveyed by exploring the natural inflection of each phrase.

A:2 **Louise Farrenc** Mouvement de valse · TB
(In the Time of a Waltz)

Charm and refinement seem to radiate from every bar of this delightful piece, in which the elegant melodic shapes and light-hearted mood of the identical outer sections contrast with a bolder middle section in the dominant key. Nimble fingerwork and a sense of fun will help to bring this little-known dance to life.

LH practice, differentiating between the sustained dotted crotchets and lighter, detached chords, would be a useful starting point for addressing balance in the outer sections. The RH semiquavers in these bars need a light, clean finger action. Practising them with dotted rhythms or staccato might help your student to gain control and evenness. Consistent fingering is vital here, especially for the arpeggio patterns in bars 13–15. In the middle section, a weightier touch, supported by firm fingers, will provide definition to the RH chords in bars 17–23. In bars 25–8, longer notes should be given their full value, while springing off the chords in bars 32–5 will project the short phrases.

Thinking in four- and eight-bar phrases, with no undue stress on each main beat, will create a sense of flow in the outer sections. Crisp staccato detail and tapered phrase endings will capture the light-hearted mood, while the melodic shapes can be highlighted by gentle hairpins. Care will be needed to maintain rhythmic consistency at the transition to the middle section. The quavers (bars 18, 20 and similar) can be detached here, before a well-graded diminuendo – perhaps with a slight slackening of pace in bar 38 – heralds the return to the opening material.

⎣A:3⎦ G. F. Handel Allegro in F ⓉⒷ

The value of practising scales is nowhere more evident than in this spirited, joyful piece! Ascending and descending scale patterns in both hands drive the music forwards, while phrasing and articulation lend elegance and poise to the dance rhythms. Listening to the sound of the harpsichord, most probably the instrument this piece was written for, would be the best way to convey to your student the brilliant, incisive attack needed for a convincing and stylish performance.

Evenness in fast scale figures is likely to be the main technical challenge. Smooth thumb turns, without dropping the wrist, will prevent any unwanted accents in the RH ascending and LH descending figures. Feeling each main beat will help to stabilise the semiquaver patterns, while crisp fingerwork, each digit released clearly, will provide definition to each note. A few rhythms need particular care – especially the crotchet in bar 10 and the RH pick-up after the bass chord in bar 11 (and elsewhere).

A suitable tempo will be one that captures the elegant mood while allowing clarity in all the musical detail. Well-shaped slurred quavers characterise some first beats, whereas elsewhere detached quavers and crotchets would give buoyancy to the texture. Lighter second and third beats, especially in the bars with quavers, will further help to convey the dance character. The suggested terraced dynamics mirror the sequences as the tonality progresses towards the D minor cadence at bars 15–16; a similar pattern, starting *mp* at bar 19, shapes the final section.

⎣B:1⎦ Valerie Capers Billie's Song ⓈⒼ

A good introduction to the jazz style of this piece would be to listen to some recordings pianist and singer Valerie Capers made with her jazz trio. An inspiring film about her early musical life is easily available to view online. Students with a feel for the genre will enjoy exploring the relative qualities of dissonance in this piece's jazz harmonies, with tones or semitones added to major and minor chords to give greater warmth or piquancy.

Initial discoveries to make with your student might include the changed effect of the chord in bar 1 when it returns in bar 3 over a different bass note; the timbre of bar 5, where C major and D minor chords are superimposed; and the harmonic brightness of the chords at the start of bars 4 and 6. Armed with these ideas, your student can choose an appropriate touch or weight for each chord, caressing the warm sounds and giving projection to more dissonant harmonies.

Few dynamics are printed, but the piece requires a constantly varying palette of tonal colours. To bring these off *con moto*, as marked, the performance will need a sense of forward direction, adding momentum and shape to the phrases. The outline melody in bars 10–12 contains unchanging repeated steps, interesting only for the ability of the player to shape them in response to the chords below. A richly resonant Neapolitan chord in bar 23, followed by lightly dropped crotchets into the resolution of the final bar, will give a stylish end.

B:2 Cécile Chaminade Idylle (SG)

The title 'Idylle' might inspire images of pleasant countryside, an imaginary paradise or a happy situation – perhaps a romance – that may not last. Whatever image your student prefers, a peaceful mood prevails in the music, with just tinges of regret or impermanence suggested by the expressive G♯ in bar 11 and the more restless, swooping melody and chromatic harmonies of the middle section (bars 17–32).

In finding a singing sound for the melody, a little extra squeezing pressure downwards into the keys, through the fingerpads, should be sufficient to project extra resonance without causing unwanted lumps of sound on each quaver. For the dotted crotchets, the tone might also need the weight of the hand, supported by relaxed control from the forearm. When adding the LH, the balance should favour the melody, allowing the accompaniment to sit inconspicuously below. This balance will provide an opportunity to create the required *dolce* sound in a gentle melodic touch that is sweet in character, but just firm enough to sing out.

Once a cantabile tone has been developed, a subtle arching contour can be sought so that individual RH notes do not protrude. The marked pedalling is only one of many options. Your student may prefer a more legato approach, where the pedal is raised when a new harmony is sounded and then immediately replaced – particularly in bars 7, 15 and 17–20. Alternatively, shorter dabs of pedal matching the pattern of the LH broken chords could give a lighter effect, although this would require the RH fingers to sustain the melodic legato reliably. A combination of both approaches might provide variety for the performance.

B:3   P. I. Tchaikovsky   La nouvelle poupée (The New Doll)

This piece from Tchaikovsky's *Album pour enfants* would suit a player with a small physique: there are no large stretches and the pedal is not required to convey the music's sound-world or character. A good memory and/or keen sense of keyboard geography would be beneficial, as the RH shifts position frequently. That said, the two opening four-bar phrases recur, which limits the amount of new material to be located.

Although the piece may look quite simple on the page, it presents a technical challenge rather like patting one's head while rubbing one's stomach. The RH paired quavers (from bar 18) need a down-up hand action to give weight to the slurred note and a delicate float back to normal wrist height for the shorter second note. By contrast, the LH pairs of quavers – always double notes – are both lightly detached, allowing the silences to play their part consistently. Playing the last note of each LH pair slightly softer would add a graceful feel.

Once these details of touch have been mastered hands together, the music's overall shape adds another dimension to the performance. Unusually, the entire piece is built from four-bar phrases, so Tchaikovsky's requested dynamic shading (or a convincing alternative) is especially necessary to avoid predictability. Although both hands will be involved in this endeavour, it will be important to maintain a suitable balance, with the LH always a little softer than the RH.

C:1   Béla Bartók   Pentatonic Tune

Bartók's pieces for children contain some characterful gems, and the fact that he has written a complete composition using only five different notes is surely awesome! There is a harmonic thief in the midst, however – a chance for some musical detective work.

The piece is not without significant challenges. The athletic jumps from bars 32 onwards, particularly in the LH, will need preparation and some 'shadow jumping'. There are also three main technical elements to be mastered: two different staccato touches and a characterful ease in playing the grace notes. The bright, *marcato* LH staccatos need a confident and decisive bounce from the wrist into the key, onto active fingertips. The lighter RH chords are best played from the surface of the key, drawing in slightly flatter fingers towards the hand with an almost trampoline-like bounce from the bottom of the action. The grace notes need to be humorously tucked in; your student could practise playing them together with the main note at first, then gently separate them.

The character of the piece is clearly festive and witty, and maybe dance-like, but the narrative is up to the performer and a good interpretation will be inspired by a vivid image or storyline. Bold dynamic contrasts and plenty of shaping are essential, as is a good control of the balance between the hands to let the melody through. Encourage your student to be playful and subtle with the written tempo changes, noticing in particular the '(*non rit.*)' at the end – the joke's final punchline.

[C:2] George Nevada Ninette's Musette

Beguiling charm, elegance and a naive innocence permeate this delightful waltz-like dance, which perhaps has its roots in the French accordion music of the bal musette.

The technical challenges lie in the lightness of touch needed for the LH chords on the second (and third) beats, as well as in the expressive independence of the RH melody. Encourage your student to think of the LH in an anticlockwise, semicircular motion, dropping into the fifth finger and then, with lateral movement, pivoting to the chord with a gentle lift. Holding the bass note underneath with the finger (as marked from bar 17) will enable a slower and more blended pedal change. In the RH, it may help your student to think of bars 25–32 as (for instance) two clarinets, perhaps balancing to the top in bars 29–32. Practising these RH phrases initially with two hands will help train the ear to listen to the underneath parts. A subtle balance between the hands is also crucial throughout. As an exercise, stop at the end of the second beat in each bar, with the pedal held, and check the chord isn't louder than the bass note and that the LH overall isn't louder than the melody note.

For grace and buoyancy, allow the music a flowing but flexible one in a bar, and a slight lilt too (just a subtle elongation of the first beat at times). The melody needs exquisite shaping throughout, and your student could explore a little more dynamic variety than marked: a *pp* echo in bars 6–8 works really well, for instance. After the dal segno, aim for a lovely, dreamy *rit.* at the end.

[C:3] Florence B. Price Ticklin' Toes

With its rag-like opening and hoedown middle section, the music's humour shines through quirky rhythms and quick changes of character.

A fearless and confident LH accompaniment is needed in the opening, so I would start with this and perhaps encourage your student to learn the first 15 bars (and the similar passage in bars 33–40) from memory. This will allow them to focus on the playfulness of the RH melody. The embellishments in the fiddle-like melody of bars 17–24 need to be tucked in, almost as if played accidentally, which can initially be disconcerting. Learning the melody without them at first (making sure the correct fingers are used) will help the memory; equally, playing all the notes as a chord cluster will help the fingers to remember the physical shapes. Releasing the weight of the arm into the held minims in bars 29 and 30 will give the sonority to the top notes.

Clear articulation and clarity of tone will lift the notes off the page in this cheerful and witty piece; no pedal is needed until the end. Include the quirky accents – the marked phrasing works well – but don't overemphasise these initially: bolder, more flat-footed accents can wait until bars 29–32. Pedal at the ready, students can let their fingers go in bars 57–61 (the semiquavers are not difficult once the patterns are known) – an enthusiastic burst of energy before a final joyous cheer for the band!

GRADE 5

A:1 **Domenico Cimarosa** Allegro (SG)

The Italian composer Domenico Cimarosa was famed for his comic operas. Exploring one of these online (e.g. the Overture or Act 1, Scene 5 aria from *L'Olimpiade*) would help your student to absorb the composer's musical style before they approach this effervescent Allegro. They could also listen to 'La Danza' by Cimarosa's younger compatriot Gioachino Rossini, which resembles this Allegro in its joy and energy, as well as in several musical features.

A useful technical tip is to play the opening Cs as an octave in the LH, to remove any uncertainty in placing the following, important RH note. The RH figurations and groups of repeating notes will require a carefully checked fingering scheme, whether this is the printed one or another that better suits the player's hand. Practising the melodic quavers hands separately, in short groups and in different rhythms, would be a good way to gain technical security so that clarity and accuracy are assured in performance.

No articulation is included in this edition, although a little variety in this respect will add vitality. The LH broken chords would work well if kept legato, whereas cadential leaps (e.g. in bars 14 and 30) would benefit from being detached. The RH (and melodic LH bars) can mostly be played legato, slurring quavers in threes or sixes. Where RH quavers are a 3rd or 5th apart (e.g. in bars 14 and 30, and in the end parts of bars 32–41), a stylish option exists to slur the first quaver of the half bar to the second, and to detach the second and third quavers.

Decisions regarding balance between the hands and dynamic shading will help your student to develop a convincing interpretation, especially where phrases or patterns are repeated. The grace notes require agility and precision and would probably be best placed stylishly on the beat (as shown in the score) rather than before it, but whichever is chosen, they should match one another in rhythm. The interrupted cadence into bar 65 and the semitones in bars 65–7 are dramatic highlights, needing tonal contrast and plenty of musical shape to set up a rousing close.

A:2 **Joseph Haydn** Minuet and Trio (SG)

Formerly an elegant court dance in three time, the minuet gradually became used in purely instrumental music of the Baroque and Classical eras. Haydn's symphonies each contain a minuet; listening to some of these will show how varied articulation and dynamic shading creates elegance for the genre. These ideas are directly transferable to performance of his piano minuets and will add interest and vitality.

The repeated RH notes (e.g. in bars 1–2 and 9–11) may result in rushed trip-lets just before them; a change of finger between the identical notes will be helpful, with extra practice to gain reliability. Ornaments are most effective when performed with a singing tone and in a melodic fashion, without sud-denness. If the suggested sextuplet realisations for trills prove too busy for full control, a simple turn could be a good solution, if musically played. The LH octave G (bar 5) is one of the Minuet's special beauties, but the hand should be ready in place during the preceding rest, to control its tone with warmth and confidence.

A clear feel for the phrasing will help to convey the style and bring the music to life. The opening presents two four-bar phrases, full of melodic and rhyth-mic invention. From bar 9 come a pair of two-bar phrases, like a question and answer, so any dynamic scheme that reflects this will be ideal. The phrasing of the Trio is slightly different, with an opportunity for dynamic drama in bars 37–40 where it unexpectedly divides into single bars, changing key rap-idly and leading to the climax of the piece. The da capo could offer a chance for further variety in the dynamic scheme.

A:3 **Chee-Hwa Tan** Jester's Jig (SG)

While the title of this flamboyant piece could helpfully lead students to seek out images of a Medieval court jester, with brightly coloured costume and cap bearing two bells, the music itself was inspired by the much later Baroque gigue. 'Jester's Jig' is the finale of a suite in which each dance includes a dis-guised quotation from the song 'Happy birthday', so early practice sessions might be enlivened by searching for fragments of that tune (hint: look in the second half!).

The lean texture of the writing would suggest little or no use of pedal and the neatest possible articulation of fingers in the semiquavers. There are a few hazardous corners: the LH moves around the keyboard quite athletically in the first half, and careful positioning of the fifth finger will be needed to main-tain accuracy in bars 3, 5–6, 9–10 and 11–12). In the second half, the RH crosses briefly over the LH in most bars; smudges on landing would spoil the line, so a rapid action for the leap should allow a millisecond of security time for checking the target note prior to sounding it.

Capturing the requested flamboyance will be key to a polished performance. The offbeat accents, played cheekily but not harshly, help to convey wit and rhythmic energy, while memorising parts of the piece may help your student to achieve its athletic qualities with confidence. The second half, built partly on descending triads, would benefit from a reticent LH and a bold sense of momentum. Any discovered quotations from 'Happy birthday' might be given a little extra emphasis to project the joke, but it is interesting that the composer does not highlight them with musical details.

B:1 **Heinrich Hofmann** Minnelied (Love Song)

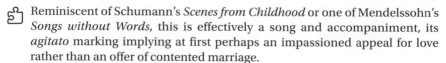

Reminiscent of Schumann's *Scenes from Childhood* or one of Mendelssohn's *Songs without Words*, this is effectively a song and accompaniment, its *agitato* marking implying at first perhaps an impassioned appeal for love rather than an offer of contented marriage.

Whatever the interpretation, a successful performance relies on a well-projected cantabile line unhindered by the semiquaver accompaniment. This is made particularly challenging as it is the thumb that controls the potentially intrusive 'in between' notes. Slow listening work will be needed to develop the control, exaggerating the overall balance with a strong tune and the most subtle of repeated notes underneath. Your student might start by playing the tune alone and then, keeping a hanging weight behind the melody fingers (transferred legato from note to note), play the thumb independently and quietly until the control becomes second nature. Rotation is not helpful here as it will throw the weight to the softer notes. Bars 24–9 feel like a rather grumpy intervention, but a relaxed drop into the keys will absorb any edge and keep the tone warm.

The piece will warm up further with greater use of the pedal but requires nothing more than the most minimal of damper lift on each quaver. It could easily sound over-pedalled, so it's important that the fingers do the legato in the top and bottom lines, to allow the pedal independence and for it to adjust as necessary.

As always with songs, encourage your student to use a narrative and make up some words to inspire and inform the musical shaping. The 'why won't you marry me?' moment in bars 13–14 instantly suggests taking some time into and out of the top note, and what might be interjections of laughter in the final bars show that happy endings are possible.

B:2 **Bernadette Marmion** Wind in the Willows

This is a lilting, lyrical, pastoral miniature full of riverbanks and sunshine with just a hint of adventure later on.

The 'tune and accompaniment' texture needs an excellent control of balance and an awareness that the rising LH arpeggio figures need to decrescendo as they ascend to avoid intruding into the melody. Adding a legato pedal change on every dotted-crotchet beat will warm the harmonies but work effectively only if the LH is light and well out of the way, otherwise it will quickly sound over-pedalled; balance and pedal are inextricably linked. Notes-wise, I would be tempted to head straight to bars 15–18 as these are the least predictable, with a hint of misadventure in the unexpected harmonies. Bars 13–14 are also worth early consideration, to bring out the LH melody.

Musically, the choice of tempo is important. Students might think of a gently rocking boat on a calm river, the pulse unhurried, then focus on shaping the two-bar RH phrases but always looking to say something different in the broader dynamic contexts. Whether conveying the p echo in bars 3–4 or the dramatic crescendo in bars 15–16, the performance needs plenty of inspired narrative. Though it's not marked, your student might consider taking a little time into the wonderful surprise of the RH diminished chord in bar 25, before all is resolved and the boat sleepily moors in the evening sunshine.

B:3   Dorothy Pilling   Philomela

Philomela is a Greek mythological figure who is transformed into a nightingale. Her mournful song permeates this music, its mood signalled by the *piangevole* (plaintive) marking at the start, birdsong-like embellishments and Impressionistic harmonies. The importance of understanding the title is evident in this poignant and hauntingly melancholy piece.

The melodic line has an improvisatory quality, exquisitely shaped and expressed across a gentle, warm, pedalled chordal accompaniment. Any searching for notes in the LH will affect the natural flow, so I would start by learning it hands separately (without pedal) to ensure that the physical movements from chord to chord are memorised. Playing each chord staccato, then moving the hand quickly to 'shadow' the next one before playing it in time, will help train the brain to think forwards.

The pedal needs a slow, blended change where marked, but students with small hands should consider bars 17 and 34, where the bass notes of the spread chords should be played with the melody note to enable a legato pedal and support of the harmony. Those with larger hands can start the spread earlier if the bass notes can be held with the fingers.

The beautiful, songlike RH melody needs flexibility, a seamless legato and communicative storytelling. Students should avoid accents after longer held notes – in bar 2, for instance, matching the sound of the (then much softer) preceding A before building again to the next bar. The *sf* markings should be treated as expressive arrival points, not accents, the composer just pointing out that the top of the phrase is not the first beat. Be bold in the f in bar 25 and leave room later for the most delicate and dreamlike pp. The ending brings a golden opportunity to explore the effect of the *una corda*, the major tonality a glimpse of a happier future.

C:1   Mike Cornick   In the Groove

The bright, upbeat feel to this piece is likely to make it a hot favourite with many candidates. Contrasts of articulation contribute to the character of the melody, which mostly mirrors the shape of the LH 7th chords, while accents serve to highlight the syncopated rhythms. Listening to famous swing musicians, such as Louis Armstrong and Duke Ellington, might inspire your student to capture the rhythmic spontaneity underpinned by a spot-on sense of pulse that is the key to bringing this style fully to life.

Discovering common notes between the LH chords will help to secure the shapes. Care is needed to give full value to tied notes, while ensuring that all notes sound in four-note chords; notes should be joined with the fingers, where possible, in the slurred figures. Establishing exactly where each main beat begins would be a good starting point for understanding the rhythm. Playing a scale with swing quavers may help, as might the fun rhythmic game of tapping the RH line with one hand while maintaining a crotchet beat with the other.

The composer indicates two accent symbols. Most serve to anticipate barlines, while the symbol used in bar 8 (and elsewhere) implies a sharper, surprise attack. Care will be needed in pacing the chords in bars 7–8, and the rests in bars 13 and 14 should be given full value. Contrasts of articulation between legato and staccato will add definition to the RH line, and slurs can be highlighted by tapering the LH chords. Carefully judged dynamic levels will allow full impact to the final bars, while a sharp attack on the last note of bar 16b and a laid-back final chord add further interest to the ending.

C:2 D. B. Kabalevsky Scherzo (TB)

Dmitry Kabalevsky's many pieces aimed at the learner combine attractiveness with a serious technical and musical purpose. Here is an excellent staccato study carefully concealed within a lively, dance-like character piece, perfect for a student with small hands. The athleticism and melodic twists and turns provide fun for the player, and although the overall dynamic level does not rise above *mf*, frequent hairpins ensure that musical interest is always maintained.

Removing the added challenge of playing staccato in the initial stages will help your student to establish note and fingering patterns. This may be their first encounter with this speed (and amount) of staccato, so some preparatory training on a scale or five-finger exercise may be necessary, using a light finger touch with well-curved digits. Although a one-in-a-bar impetus is the ultimate aim, slow practice, feeling three clear beats in a bar, will develop control in the quaver movement. Unwanted hesitations can be prevented by preparing the hand crossings in bars 22 and 24 during the rests, and 'blocking' the B minor triad figures in bars 34–5 will establish the shapes.

Establishing a maintainable tempo that allows clarity in the detail will be crucial for a convincing performance. While two instances of *mf* act as high points in the delicate overall tonal palette, elsewhere surges in tone serve to mirror the melodic contours. Despite the LH's largely supportive role, its accented 3rds play an important part in underpinning the hemiola in bars 9–12. Only the slightest hint of a *rit.* is needed to herald the repeat of the opening material at bar 13, while the sparkle and wit of the final *leggierissimo* is best served by resisting any slackening of pace.

[C:3] **David A. T. Önaç** A Distant Star in the Stillness   (TB)

The sheer pleasure of exploring a wide keyboard range is likely to be one of the chief attractions of this atmospheric piece. The slow-moving chords, jazz-inspired, provide a sense of space and mystery that perfectly evokes the vastness of the universe. Imagination and keen listening skills will be vital for creating atmosphere in this seemingly elusive style, while a confident sense of pulse will ensure a sense of structure.

Accustoming the ear to the musical language can be assisted in the early stages by playing each note individually from the bass upwards, followed by the whole chord. An understanding of tonality would help with note learning in bars 14–22, as E flat major gives way to E major midway through bar 19; as always, students with small hands should feel free to omit the occasional inner chord note where necessary. Clapping the RH patterns while maintaining a regular pulse will help to establish rhythmic stability, and your student may find it beneficial to write in exactly where each main beat occurs.

The pedal, used throughout and cleared fully on each change, plays a key role in sustaining the texture, while arm weight, supported by flexible wrists and firm fingers, provides sonority and warmth at all dynamic levels. Highlighting the top notes will create focus in the melodic line, and weight marks serve to further underline special moments. The high G-D motif, first heard in bars 1–2, provides recurring glimpses of the title's 'distant star', and a sense of space can be conveyed in the outer sections by giving full value to all long notes. Musical tension builds midway from bar 14, leading inevitably to a rich climax in bar 23, further enhanced by the generous upward spread.

GRADE 6

A:1 **Stephen Heller** Prelude in C sharp minor

This charming and delightful prelude by a French musical poet is just one of many glorious yet sometimes overlooked miniatures from Heller. As with many of his small-scale piano compositions, it's much harder than it looks, but the musical rewards are huge. Heller's music is Romantic to the core, so some familiarity with the piano music of more well-known composers such as Schumann and Chopin will certainly help your student to understand the idiom and gain a sense of the subtle rubato needed.

Technical ease and subtle dynamic control of the LH accompaniment in the opening figures will be the linchpin in communicating a dance-like elegance and beauty. Using an anticlockwise, circular motion – falling into the bass note, keeping the wrist low while travelling to the first chord then adding a light lift on the final quaver – will help to establish the root of the harmony and provide a graceful lift. Controlling the RH runs needs careful persuasion into the fingers, avoiding an accent on the first semiquaver. From bar 17, students should treat the RH as couplets, dropping into the top note and holding it until the chord has sounded, then lightly lifting; the accents here are just to point out the melodic line, nothing more.

It may help to consider the RH runs as an alluring melody, allowing a natural and relaxed fluid flexibility to the pulse and highlighting to the listener the delightfully unexpected change of harmonies such as those in bar 6. Bar 7 might be a slightly light-hearted aside to break the melancholy mood. Students should think of bar 40 onwards as a series of pedalled harmonies (the semiquaver movement hidden without too much brightness and articulation), perhaps creating the impression of gradually waking from a dream as the patterns descend, with a fragment of a memory in the final bars.

A:2 **Elisabetta de Gambarini** Giga in D

Students will have encountered Baroque dances in their earlier repertoire, so this is a wonderful opportunity to discuss the different character of each dance, and perhaps also to introduce the idea of a collection of dances, with an eye to the future and the Bach and Handel suites. The gigue itself takes on subtle differences in character depending on its nationality, which might provide further scope for exploration.

This cheeky and optimistic Giga requires fleetness of finger and a subtle exploration of shape using both articulation and dynamic shading. It is almost impossible to separate interpretation from technique at any stage, so before finalising the fingering discuss and decide on the articulation. I would avoid a uniform couplet phrasing of the first two quavers in every group of three, as this would inevitably provide an emphasis on almost every beat. Instead, look for longer phrases, such as bars 25–7, where your student could phrase the first two quavers of the RH as a couplet but then keep the quavers detached until the dotted crotchet, giving the melody a forward momentum across the bar-line. Then decide on a fingering to enhance the phrasing, matching the chosen phrasing between the hands where the figurations are the same.

Technically, the phrasing and articulation are so much easier if the hands themselves dance – a relaxed wrist, dropping gently where the notes are phrased in couplets and rising to lighten the shorter notes; a gentle bounce from the wrist for articulated phrases; and using the ends of the fingers to give sparkle and brilliance at speed.

Keeping the Giga on its toes, full of subtle surprises and effervescent, is the key to a successful performance. A good choice of tempo is also fundamental: too fast and the detail is obscured, too slow and the buoyancy is lost. A gentle rise and fall in the dynamic is always effective but experiment with terraced dynamics as well, particularly through the sequences. A gentle placing of the final notes will add charm and elegance.

A:3 Friedrich Kuhlau Allegro AW

This colourful and absorbing sonatina movement is full of operatic song and dramatic changes of mood, reflecting not only Kuhlau's operatic writing but also his love of Beethoven's music, which he championed during the composer's lifetime.

The technical challenges are mainly twofold: balancing the Alberti bass and the songlike melody, and controlling the fast scalic runs. Students could practise the opening LH accompaniment with the whole chord held gently down, lifting the fingers just enough to play the notes and convey a gentle, harmonic sonority. If they then want a bit more energy in the articulation, they can lift the fingers a little more, giving varied control of the dynamic and rhythmic excitement. The scalic melodies need shape and direction, so encourage students to float into the runs with a light arm, avoiding any first-beat accents. Unevenness can often be remedied by some rhythm and accent work, but consistent fingering is essential for this to be effective.

Musically, the performance needs a narrative – a slightly coquettish opening, perhaps, the repeated notes never lifeless but growing through to the next bar, followed (from upbeat to bar 9) by a more robust and perhaps pompous reply from the second onstage actor, which clearly provokes a rather grumpy change of mood in bar 13! Don't be scared here to use some pedal for rich LH octaves, keeping the agitated triplets just a little less obvious to help the sense of line. It would be very easy to become undemanding and just play the notes, particularly in passages such as bars 41–5 with its single marked dynamic. Instead, encourage your student always to consider the interpretation, experimenting with contrast and colour inspired by an operatic scene of their imagination.

B:1 R. N. Dett Honey (TB)

The key to a convincing performance of this piece lies in a wholehearted response to the changes of mood. Understanding the phrase structure, with its four- or eight-bar units, will help your student to mould the sections – which range from easy-going swagger to intense passion and finally playfulness – into a coherent whole. Apart from the term of endearment suggested by the title, the composer leaves scope for the performer to imagine their own scenario.

Some groundwork on rhythm may be necessary, practising the syncopated bars strictly in time while feeling the main beats. Small hands may need to omit some inner thumb notes in larger stretches, although all notes should be played in the LH 10th chords in bar 34 and elsewhere, spreading upwards if necessary. While some pedalling is indicated, further options are possible: for instance, generous use would enhance the dreamy atmosphere in bars 41–4, while your student may prefer to leave all the semiquavers in the final four bars unpedalled.

Grace notes placed just before the bar-line add a little urgency to the opening RH figures, as they lead naturally towards the climax midway through the eight-bar phrase. The upward shift to A minor at bar 9 seems to offer a moment of even greater tenderness, whereas a rich cantabile tone, savouring every melodic note and pause, will capture the impassioned mood of the *meno mosso* (bars 17–20). Perhaps the suitor finally plucks up courage to declare their feelings, after earlier hints, at the *Molto meno mosso* in bar 29? Further lingerings follow, with some delicious harmonies to enjoy before a matter-of-fact flourish, well in time, brings the proceedings to a humorous finish.

B:2 Enrique Granados Vals poético (Poetic Waltz) (TB)

The mixture of tenderness and passion in this piece make it an ideal vehicle for developing your student's expressive range. Switches between minor and major give poignancy to the musical language, while the frequent lingering at phrase ends seems to evoke the memory of a distant waltz. Perhaps the composer is allowing us a glimpse into his own feelings, maybe with a tinge of regret for times past.

Developing a warm cantabile, using the weight of the arm behind firm, responsive fingers, is a key requirement in the learning stage. Although the melody remains at the top of the texture throughout, the importance of inner and bass notes for creating movement and harmonic interest – especially in the rising phrase in bars 11–13 – should also be acknowledged. A lateral swing of the arm, with a flexible wrist, will assist the widely spaced arpeggio figures in bars 33–6 (and subsequently), and small hands may prefer to use a thumb on the second note (D) in bars 36 and 44. The ear is the best guide to pedalling choices, the frequency of lifts determined by the speed of harmonic change. Awareness of the pedal's responsiveness, especially on an unfamiliar instrument, will be crucial for ensuring clarity at each change.

Your student should feel free to explore the natural ebb and flow of each eight-bar phrase, allowing time to be suspended at each *rall*. Shifts between minor and major offer scope for subtle mood changes within the predominantly quiet dynamic. A firm bass line will reinforce the RH line at the *con passione* in bars 27–9, while the supporting LH arpeggios play their part in giving full impact to the short-lived F sharp major climax at bar 33.

B:3 **Felix Mendelssohn** Venetianisches Gondellied (TB) (Venetian Gondola Song)

Many musicians and writers have been inspired by Venice, with its gondolas that transport passengers smoothly and luxuriously through the city's waterways. The barcarolle, a song in compound time traditionally sung by gondoliers, is transformed here into an instrumental form, with the 'vocal' sections, often in duet, framed by an introduction and postlude.

Developing a warm cantabile touch for the melodic lines, with the fingers joining the RH double notes wherever possible, is a key requirement in the learning stage. Distinguishing between melody and accompaniment in the RH in bars 18–24 needs care – your student may find it helpful to isolate the top line before adding the inner detail here. In the LH, an arc-like movement of the forearm for negotiating the larger leaps will help to prevent any unwanted bumps. While legato pedalling, changing on each new harmony, suits the predominantly sustained texture, a more airy feel can be created in bars 25–33 by reducing the amount of pedal to short dabs on the bass notes.

A two-in-a-bar lilt, with light offbeat quavers, will establish the calm motion of a gondola. Although the RH provides the melodic interest throughout, sufficiently prominent bass notes on the main beats serve to establish the harmonies. Subtle shaping will give direction and interest to the predominantly quiet dynamic, and a change of texture can be created by lightly detaching the semi-staccato notes at bar 25 (and elsewhere). The *pp* in bar 22 offers a special moment, heightened by the diminished 7th harmony and extended pedal indication. The climax at bar 32 as C minor is reached proves short-lived, after which a more fragmented melody and waning energy bring this imaginary journey subtly to a close.

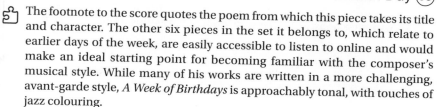

C:1 R. R. Bennett The Child that is Born on the Sabbath Day (SG)

The footnote to the score quotes the poem from which this piece takes its title and character. The other six pieces in the set it belongs to, which relate to earlier days of the week, are easily accessible to listen to online and would make an ideal starting point for becoming familiar with the composer's musical style. While many of his works are written in a more challenging, avant-garde style, *A Week of Birthdays* is approachably tonal, with touches of jazz colouring.

Although the lean texture, octave writing and triad shapes will make for fairly rapid note-learning, students may find it quite hard to present the semi-quaver groups with rhythmic precision and even tone at a suitably quick tempo. Neighbouring notes and the swap from one hand to the other are especially tricky; these would benefit from slow practice in different rhythms, short-long and long-short, always listening for equality in finger articulation. As the tempo is increased, fluidity of wrist movements can be explored, enabling a relaxed sweep of the hands to support the fingerwork. Dropping slightly into the stronger half of the bar and lifting lightly up from the keys at the end of each six-note group may help your student to find agility and sparkle.

Refinement in tonal shading will enhance the quavers; staccatos can be firmly weighted or delicate in touch, for variety. The short groups of legato quavers (e.g. in bars 11–13) will be more interesting if musical shapes are copied between the hands, the most effective dynamic shading of each group discovered by experimentation. Making artistic decisions such as this should give your student a sense of positive ownership of the music, according to their choices.

C:2 Elissa Milne Indigo Moon

This stunning, hypnotic piece is a gift for any pianist who relishes minor keys, syncopation and chords with added notes. The composer has been fascinated since childhood with the way that chords, and small changes to them, can subtly alter a mood. As a teacher and encourager of young musicians, she has created a 'Challenge' experience to explore how chords actually work. The melodic material of 'Indigo Moon' is minimal, if beautiful; it is harmony and rhythm that make the piece so memorable.

There are a few rhythmic challenges to bear in mind. Many bars contain syncopation midway; it is important not to rush here, especially before demisemiquavers, as in bars 1 and 3. Other places that will require poise to avoid undermining the pulse are the more spacious bars (e.g. bars 6, 7 and 22) and bar 23, where the crescendo might lead to accidental hurrying. In fact, a firm pulse throughout is essential for this piece to work, even if occasional and momentary lingering over the player's favourite notes might add to the expressive effect in performance. The music also contains some slightly awkward position-shifts (e.g. bar 9 into bar 10), where a good feel for keyboard geography will assist your student in keeping a smooth flow.

Decisions about pedalling will be key to communicating the sound-world of the music. Changing at the start of each bar will often fit the harmony well. Many chords include a semitone as part of their colouring (e.g. in bars 1 and 10) and these can be allowed to resonate within one pedal. However, some more melodic semitone steps in, for example, bars 3 and 7, and the LH 7ths in bar 8 may need a pedal change to avoid smudging. Careful listening while experimenting should lead your student to stylish choices in this respect. Milne has provided many dynamic details which will add dramatic intensity to the playing.

[C:3] Oscar Peterson Jazz Exercise No. 2

Finding the groove in jazz music – which is a feel, rather than a quantifiable technique – could prove challenging to a student used to the precision and smooth flow of J. S. Bach or Mozart, for example. Listening to Monty Alexander perform Stevie Wonder's 'Isn't She Lovely', and to Oscar Peterson himself in 'Tangerine', might prove helpful. If listeners are found to be foot-tapping or wanting to dance while listening to a performance of this Jazz Exercise, then the player has found the groove!

Technical work with your student will focus on rhythm and fingering. Quavers and dotted quavers should both be swung, giving a looser feel to the rhythm than in classical style. There is much work for the RH fifth and fourth fingers, partly in terms of accuracy but also, importantly, in providing the (unmarked) characteristic offbeat accents. These need an emphatic sound but not a harsh one. Pairs of semiquavers (bars 12 and 24) can be played more or less rhythmically as written, with an ornamental feel to the touch rather than a purposefully melodic sound.

To interpret the style convincingly, percussive articulation, emphasising offbeat notes especially at the beginning and end of a phrase, will help to create the syncopated, choppy flow that gives the music vitality. The LH can boost the effect wherever its notes fall before the beat.

Although there are no marked dynamics or other expressive details, phrase-shaping and some tonal surprises will be beneficial. The latter could include highlighting the rising chromatic RH 3rds in bars 9–10; the false relation between the RH A♯ and LH A♮ in bar 12; and the marvellous LH D♯ that sets the middle section underway in bar 17. While the major key and energetic mood suggest a predominantly projected tone, a few moments of quiet, as if sharing a secret, could add witty touches.

GRADE 7

A:1   **Joseph Haydn** Allegro moderato   (TB)

The inventive, lively mind of the composer is particularly evident in this first movement of his Sonata in B minor. Plenty of contrasts and surprises give energy and sparkle to the music, while the tempering effect of the *moderato* within the tempo indication suggests a breadth to the pace. Listening to a recording on a fortepiano of Haydn's time would provide an aural template of that instrument's capacity for lightness and clarity within a narrower dynamic scale, qualities that can be incorporated into your student's performance on the modern instrument.

A secure sense of pulse is a primary factor in holding the structure together. The choice of tempo will be partly governed by the runs and ornaments in bars 22–4, and some rhythms will need careful measuring – in particular, the alternation of semiquavers and triplets in bars 21–5 (and bars 63–7), and rests at the ends of sections. Some additional fingerwork-training, perhaps using scales or exercises, would help agility and evenness, and supple hand and wrist movement is needed for definition at slur ends. Isolating the LH leaps, moving in advance to the new position, will aid accuracy, while busier passages at the approach to each double bar-line may need memorising.

Although the editorial dynamics are helpful, there is considerable scope for your student to explore various tonal alternatives. An awareness of the sonata-form structure, with its three main sections, will help to shape the performance. A bold tone, with clearly defined articulation and ornaments placed on (not before) the beat, will capture the arresting character at the opening, while a gentler approach, shapely in its longer lines, seems to suit the mellifluous second subject from bar 13. One can sense the composer having fun during the development after the double bar-line (bar 29) while exploring ideas presented previously. This section forms the emotional centre of the movement as it passes through various keys, before a persistently defined dotted motif leads back resolutely to the more familiar territory of the recapitulation.

A:2   **Bohuslav Martinů** Allegretto   (TB)

Martinů's lifelong fascination with rhythm is nowhere more apparent than in this piece, with its frequent shifts in metre and quaver patterns. Accentuation provides focus and drive to the constant quaver motion, while further musical interest is supplied by contrasts in articulation and dynamics. A sustainable *allegretto* pace, keeping a firm hold on the reins, is the key to a confident performance in which your student can enjoy all the musical ingredients that bring this quirky, unpredictable style to life.

Each new section, usually indicated by a change in time signature, presents its own technical issues, so it may be wise to approach them individually in the early stages of learning. Most coordination challenges are likely to occur in the opening 16 bars, so slow practice may be necessary here, perhaps initially omitting the staccato in the LH. Clarity in the RH chords in bars 37–44 can be achieved by a hand staccato, supported by a flexible wrist, while additional forearm weight will be needed for the necessary attack in the final line. Elsewhere, however, greater agility may be achieved by a finger staccato. A vertical hand movement, again flexible at the wrist, plays its part in facilitating and shaping the two-note slurs.

Imagining that they are conducting the piece, indicating the main crotchet/dotted-crotchet beats, may help your student to feel the rhythmic groupings. Frequent accents serve to emphasise the alternation between groups of two and three quavers, while some slurs further highlight the bar-lines, for example in bars 17–24. Despite the composer's relatively narrow overall dynamic range, contrast in the *f* sections can be achieved by dropping back sufficiently at the *mf* indications. Greater delicacy might be explored in bars 37–44, while smooth RH chords, with the top note sustained by the fingers, offer further textural variety in the subsequent bars. Although not marked, maintaining the crescendo through bars 67–70 will give maximum effect to the long final build-up, which begins with the *p* at bar 49.

[A:3] **Marianne von Martínez** Tempo di minuetto (TB)

This third movement from the composer's Sonata in A seems to encapsulate all the elegance and grace we associate with the eighteenth century. Although this piece was probably never intended for the ballroom, one can sense the graceful, measured gestures of the dance, unhurried yet purposeful. The binary structure, which prefigures sonata form, provides a sense of order to the music. Much of the figuration would lend itself to being played on a string instrument, an image that might help your student to capture the clean-cut style.

The main technical challenge is likely to be maintaining a consistent crotchet pulse while transitioning between quavers, triplets and semiquavers. An interactive clapping exercise might help (for example, your student switching between different rhythmic units while you maintain a steady beat), as would the occasional check with the metronome. In the large RH leaps, spotting the arrival notes in advance, moving swiftly and confidently, will prevent any unwanted hesitations. It will also help to isolate the two-note joins over bar-lines (e.g. in bars 15–16), practising the leaps in both directions, perhaps occasionally without looking at the keyboard. Initially removing the ornaments may be necessary for establishing a stable pulse. Although the decorations are integral to the style, your student should feel free to modify any troublesome patterns; for example, groups of four semiquavers might be a simpler option in bar 8.

The absence of any dynamic indications provides a blank canvas for experimenting with different choices. While an awareness of the less resonant, gentler tone of the early piano should govern the overall dynamic range, contrasts that reflect changes of register (e.g. the octave switch at bar 25) might be explored. Gentle rise and fall would mirror the scalic figures at bar 15 (and elsewhere), while echo effects at phrase repetitions, for example in bars 6–7, would provide a stylish option. Further musical variety can be found in contrasts of touch: a slightly detached attack would suit the decisiveness of the opening, for instance, whereas the mellifluous triplet figures seem to suggest a smoother approach.

B:1   **Fryderyk Chopin**   Mazurka in A minor

Chopin's youthful compositions include several in the style of national dances, among them polonaises and mazurkas. A deep sadness pervades this early Mazurka in A minor, written when the composer was 17. Its sorrowful nature arises from use of the characteristically Polish Lydian mode, in which the sharpened 4th (D♯) – here, usually ornamented – adds exotic colour.

Technical work in the early stages should focus on the means to produce a ringing cantabile tone in the melody, even for the softest playing. Important elements are relaxed forearm weight, flexibility through the wrist and hand, and firm use of the soft pad under each fingertip. Matching the tone between dotted rhythms, crotchets and ornaments will require careful listening, so that the various elements combine to create a smooth, singing line.

The double 3rds and 6ths in bars 31–2 and 35–6 will benefit from matching the tone between upper and lower notes, so that all lines collaborate in expression of the myriad printed musical details. While a light precision will help to incorporate the ornamentation in these bars without disturbing the rhythmic framework, it is important that each ornamental note is heard. Again, a relaxed weight behind the hand and firm fingers will be the key to confidence in performing these tricky bars on an unfamiliar piano.

Communication of this mazurka's most beautiful moments will entail an exploration of its harmonic journey. The relative major key in bars 17–20 lifts the spirits, with F♯ and D♯ accidentals adding piquancy. Arrival in the tonic major at bar 29 gives yet greater warmth, but the chromatic harmonic shifts and rich, five-note chords in bars 37–44 will require detailed voicing of inner parts and refined tonal colouring. In contrast, the heartbreaking return to the spare, open texture and minor key of the opening material at bar 45 would suggest an especially tender touch.

Judicious use of pedal is most important in preserving melodic legato and harmonic warmth. The printed pedal markings give a basic guide to where changes might be made, but there is scope for a much more subtle approach in expressing the music's poetry. For example, lifting the pedal as indicated on the third beat of most bars would lead to frequent choppiness in sound, whereas lightly and briefly replacing the pedal at these points will add colour and smoothness. In the major key middle section, longer periods of pedalling are occasionally suggested, although some pedal is essential even where no marking is printed. The player's imagination and musical ear should be the judge.

B:2 · **Jan Freidlin** At the Evening Window

Jan Freidlin's compositions include five symphonies as well as music for seven films and several television and theatre productions. Students interested in exploring his music further might listen to the Romantic Concerto for trombone. It shares with this piece a reflective and rhythmically free nature, and the harmonic language is similarly warm, with interesting dissonant, spiky twists.

For most of this piece the notes are not hard to locate, so focus with your student on the more challenging areas of tonal control and rhythmic flexibility. The texture is lean; even where four parts are present, a truly cantabile tone (with some weight from the forearm directed to the fingertips) will be needed to help the lines sing with warmth and expression. A little pedal will be helpful, especially where repeated notes and wide leaps would otherwise break the legato flow. Changing pedal every crotchet or, where more clarity is desired, every quaver should be effective, perhaps leaving the last two bars to resonate without any change.

In the outer sections of the piece, encourage your student to explore the rubato style – with increased forward momentum balanced by a tender relaxation of the flow in each phrase – while taking care to avoid tonal unevenness. The phrasing often overlaps between the hands, so it's not always the top line that needs the most projection. Indeed, when the *Andante rubato* returns at bar 53, it is the LH that leads the way. For a convincing performance of the *Poco animato* middle section (bars 23–52), a more energetic sense of expression might join the slight increase in tempo. The wide leaps and semitone steps have a more purposeful feel here as the music builds to the climax of the piece in bar 37, its *quasi f* marking a warning against too bright a tone.

B:3 Moritz Moszkowski Calme du soir (The Calm of the Evening)

A star of the Parisian music scene in mid-life, Moszkowski was famed for his piano music and wrote more than 200 short piano pieces, many of which are used today as encores after recitals. 'Calme du soir' is Romantic in style and would suit a student who enjoys rich sonorities, touching harmonies and the opportunity to communicate a poetic atmosphere.

At first glance, the music may seem almost hymn-like in texture, yet many important melodic lines lie hidden in the lower parts. Careful listening and subtlety of touch will help students to balance the texture effectively, while legato fingering will be beneficial in bringing out the melodies. In several bars (e.g. 12 and 17–23), three or even four parts operate as soloists together, their independent lines feeling almost contrapuntal. Where not marked otherwise, pedal changes connecting each quaver would preserve the smooth, warm sound while not clouding the movement of the separate voices.

An awareness of the two-bar phrasing – starting a phrase tenderly then finding a sense of more projected forward momentum before closing it in restfulness – will help students to bring out the emotion in the music. The calm mood is perhaps disturbed by a few eddies of stiff evening breeze as the harmonic journey becomes more complex after bar 13 and the smooth flow turns agitated in bars 17–18. More activity here in phrase-shaping and dynamic detailing will give the passage dramatic contrast, leading back to the sweeter tonal colouring of the closing bars.

C:1 Christopher Norton New Kid

One of a set of jazz preludes by the composer, this engaging, fun piece is said to have a Charleston flavour, yet it seems more closely influenced by other 1920–30s fast dance styles – there's even a hint of Glenn Miller's 'In the Mood' – more Lindy hop, perhaps?

To bring the performance to life, students must cultivate not only a strong swing feel to the quavers but also a solidly underpinned pulse, excellent sense of rhythm and characterful syncopation. Practising the notes first may seem logical, but the rhythmic character is quickly lost as fingers find their way around. Instead, work with your student at the rhythm away from the piano – clapping musically and counting aloud – effectively acquiring a template upon which to hang the notes. The performance needs to be engaging and quick on its feet, so students should keep the tone quality light, bright and clear; staying on the ends of the fingers will undoubtedly help.

In performance, it is important to convey the characterful pushes (small accents) that give a swing performance its overall feel. None of these are marked on the score and may feel unfamiliar, so your student might listen to

Bill Evans's 'Freddie Freeloader' (from *You Must Believe in Spring*) for a masterclass. Idiomatic examples in 'New Kid' might be a quick, small accent on the first C; a slight emphasis on the final A♭ of the first bar; and a slight kick on the second note of bars 5 and 6.

The middle section is effectively a melodic improvisation over a four-note riff. It would be easy to let the performance become a bit musically predictable, so explore dynamic shape and contrast beyond the written markings. Overall, very little pedal is needed – just small touches to enhance the phrasing and encourage the warmth, optimism and humour.

⟨C:2⟩ **D. G. Rahbee** Prelude: Twilight

 This is a delightful and evocative prelude, conjuring images of rose-tinged horizons and distant bells. In its soundscape, if not its harmonic language, it's reminiscent of a Debussy prelude, so listening to some of these might make a good starting point for your student.

 The piece will suit larger hands. The widely spaced LH broken chords need a gentle and unobtrusive wash of sound and unobtrusive pedal changes. Those students with smaller hands will therefore need to use lots of lateral movement at the wrist around the middle note to avoid tension and help control the tone on the thumb notes; these need to be quieter than the initial bass note so that the figurations are tonally balanced on the pedal change.

The score suggests the third finger on the middle note, but I would experiment with the second too; holding the bass note under the second note is almost more important than a small leap to the top note, helping a slower pedal change while capturing the root of the harmony. Above all, your student should use whatever feels most natural.

The beginnings of the melodic phrases shouldn't have an accent but should float gently in. This is particularly tricky in bar 1, where the thumb has to tuck under quickly to the A, so it is worth some focused practice.

 This wonderful piece is effectively a musical painting, so it's important that your student has an image in mind then asks themselves what this mental picture sounds like in tone and balance. Choice of tempo is crucial; stand and reflect on the scene rather than describing it, giving it plenty of space and time. A regular bell chime would not normally suggest any rubato, but a little flexibility to the pulse around the chimes here is essential to allow a natural flow and spaciousness. Encourage students to think in a three-part texture, deciding on the dynamic range and just how much the bells come through. Shape the melodic phrases, and colour the chords to reflect the beauty of the soft, glowing light.

C:3 **Param Vir** White Light Chorale

The music of Param Vir follows a strong tradition of composers for whom pitch and harmony take on a dimension beyond conventional ideas of tonality. It's a musical language that hugely rewards those who take time to embrace its sound-world and musical philosophy, emotions and images not necessarily experienced in conventional major and minor keys. For further context, students might listen to the hauntingly compelling *Tombeau de Messiaen* by Jonathan Harvey (a former teacher of Vir).

Technically, begin by considering the RH repeated notes. For absolute control of rhythm and tone, alternation of the fingers is a must, and I would strongly suggest doing this in the 4-3-2-1 groups in bars 4–13. This also has the advantage of effectively counting the number of repeated notes as you go. In bars 14–17, the 2-1-2-1 finger pattern is needed initially to hold the top D, and you could continue with this into bar 15, but I would be tempted to change to 4-3-2-1-2 at this point. See what feels most comfortable and gives the greatest control.

The piece will benefit from work without pedal, focusing on quiet, controlled semiquavers while confidently and independently finding and playing the chords in the other hand. Encourage your student to be conscientious about the counting in bars 1–3, and the tempo relationship to what follows.

The image of a sung chorale in the chords and intense white light in the high repeated notes is a wonderful starting point for the interpretation. In the opening, think of the cavernous space of a cathedral and cherish the atmospheric, sombre sonority. The dramatic scalic run in bar 4 seems to depict a sudden beam of sunlight, shimmering while the mystical choir sing their chorale in the LH chords, with a shapely crescendo to the climax in bar 10. The RH chorale tune needs an intensity throughout, with plenty of brightness in the tone and musical direction towards the almost bell-like *ff* accent in bar 14. Students should listen sensitively to the balance and dynamic at all times; a long-held pedal can soon allow the sonority to build and become disproportionately loud.

The longer note values towards the end, coupled with the *molto rit.* marking, leave no doubt that the composer is aspiring to a very slow ending, with lots of space and time for meditation in the final notes.

GRADE 8

A:1 **J. S. Bach** Prelude and Fugue in B flat

Although the harpsichord was probably the intended instrument for this work, the toccata-like opening more readily recalls some of the composer's organ works – for example, the Prelude in A, BWV 536. Listening to this could provide a good introduction to the genre.

Technical work in the Prelude might focus on the broken chords in bars 1–10. This requires a loose rotation of the RH wrist to avoid thumb notes protruding, and a balance that favours the wonderful bass line. All demisemiquavers will need firm fingerwork and evenness of tone, which can be improved through practising in different rhythms and at different dynamic levels. In the Fugue, fingering choices should ensure control and balance of the independent lines, with a clean legato except on any quavers chosen to sound detached.

The Prelude presents students with many opportunities for interpretation. The runs in bars 11–19 can gather a sense of improvisation through a slightly flexible rhythmic flow, with the tone of the initial demisemiquaver (in bars 11, 13, 16, 18 and 19) matched to the decaying sound of the preceding crotchet. When the music arrives in bars 11, 13 and 15, the quaver rest and dotted chords should be rhythmically accurate and consistent from one line to the next, lending structure to the section overall.

The absence of marked dynamics offers your student the chance to communicate entirely personal views about the music. In this respect, there is no 'right' and very little 'wrong', except for a lack of shape and perhaps a risk of over-enthusiasm in the Prelude's strong chords: a harsh tone here will deflect from the music's majesty, whereas a rich warmth (with added pedal) is stylish. An effective dynamic scheme for the Fugue will help to convey its structure: episodes where the main part of the subject is silent can be different from those phrases where the subject is stated, for example bars 7–8, 11–12 and 15–18. A gradual crescendo might add excitement in the final lines. Phrasing and articulation of the subject itself should lead the ear towards each new bar, but the choices are many and various.

A:2 **W. A. Mozart** Allegro

This sunny first movement from the Sonata in F, K. 332, features a combination of great tunes, athletic flashes of dramatic colour, dancing elegance and irresistible chains of 7th chords. Although the music has many original features, it is worth exploring the ways in which it is typical of sonata form of that period. The standard three sections give the structure: exposition, development (bar 94) and recapitulation (bar 133). Greater understanding of the genre can be gained by exploring the first movements of sonatas by J. C. Bach and Haydn, most of which follow the same sonata-form structure but in a multitude of unique ways.

A few technically treacherous moments lie in wait. At bars 31–6, agility is required for sparkling semiquavers, yet hand coordination may be lost in the connection from the tied crotchet. Thinking ahead during the crotchet and beginning the semiquaver flourish smoothly can assist with the timing. The bars that contain cross-rhythms (49–50 and 185–6) need smoothly reticent LH triplets and expressively shaped RH dissonances and resolutions, leaning into the first quaver of each pair and lifting lightly from the second. Separate-hands work, with the metronome set to a crotchet beat, will help to avoid rhythmic uncertainty for any student lacking experience of playing 'two against three'.

Sparing use of the pedal, changing every crotchet or minim, will help to preserve the music's natural clarity. However, scalic passages and detached, dancing chords need a clean, unpedalled sound. The bars of RH double 3rds (e.g. bars 67–70) would be more stylish if kept legato through the use of well-practised, safe fingering than through any use of pedal.

Discussions about contrasts of character could be enlivened using orchestral imagery, as if painting the phrases in specific instrumental colours (inspiration for this might come from listening to the first movement of Mozart's Symphony No. 39, after the long introduction). Questions about articulation, tonal colour, balance and projection suited to each melodic or accompaniment figure might be answered, for example, by recalling the timbre of the bassoon, the expressive warmth of the violin, two energetic horns, or the delicacy of a solo flute.

A:3 **Franz Schubert** Moment musical in C sharp minor   (SG)

Schubert's *Moments musicaux* form a somewhat under-appreciated group of six short masterpieces. They are neither showy nor overtly dramatic, but their poetry is deeply touching. A student considering learning this piece could spend a happy afternoon playing through or listening to the other five, to discover the range of emotions they contain and grasp an understanding of the harmonic language.

The outer sections will need careful balance between the hands, especially in quiet phrases; a light touch for the LH staccatos will help to avoid the detached quavers becoming too dominant. The RH semiquaver figurations include a number of tricky shapes, liable to upset the seamless flow of controlled tone. A gently rotating wrist and precise finger technique would combine to create security, with any more awkward bars isolated for daily attention until reliability is gained. Practice in dotted rhythms, importantly both long-short and short-long, would help to iron out any remaining unevenness. Where your student's hand size allows, the RH 6ths in bars 68–9 (and other chordal writing in ensuing bars) should be fingered to bring out the top melody in the most smoothly singing way possible, not relying solely on the pedal for legato.

The Bach-like character of the opening suggests an absence of pedal, although small touches as it moves along would open up a more Romantic sound-world. Passages marked with slurs in the LH might be coloured more warmly, so long as harmonic changes are kept distinct. Touches of pedal every crotchet or quaver in bars 39–42, and occasionally from there until bar 60, could give subtlety of colour according to personal taste and the nature of the specific piano involved. The middle section (bars 62–101), with its lilting folk-dance rhythm, will need subtle phrasing and dynamic shaping to capture its emotional core. The offbeat accents require merely a nudge, rather than a spike of sound, to launch the momentum found in the first part of every bar while preserving the natural emphasis on downbeats. A lightened touch on the end of each bar would add a gracefully stylish nuance.

B:1 Samuel Coleridge-Taylor Impromptu in B minor

For many teachers and students, the music of Samuel Coleridge-Taylor will be unfamiliar. While in his harmonic language there are hints of English composers who helped his career, such as Elgar and Stanford, a glimpse into some recordings of this under-played composer's music would be a worthwhile adventure.

In the opening and similar bars, as well as in the middle section, the melody is at the top of the chords and needs to be clearly defined and musically shaped. If this does not come naturally to your student, a good strategy would be to half hold down the lower notes (with a relaxed arm) then, lifting the top finger slightly above the key, play the chord by focusing on the top note and dropping gently into the keys. Once the ear hears the right balance, then the 'feel' for the control can be remembered.

The pedalling needs to be well-coordinated and intuitive. There are times where it shouldn't catch the grace notes (such as the opening) but also times where it needs to do just this (e.g. bars 21–8), even if for only half the bar. Small hands may be unable to hold on to the bottom notes of the spread chords in bars 55 and 56 long enough to help catch them in the pedal and/or avoid a gap in the melodic line. Your student could either start the RH and LH arpeggiated chords together or hold the previous melody note over the spread chord, including it in the pedal change; it will not be obvious and will help the legato line.

A personal and expressive voice is needed to communicate the charm and mood of this truly delightful and engaging piece, which is perhaps incidental music in the opening then songlike in its middle section. Students needn't be too literal when observing the markings, therefore; instead, encourage them to interpret the detail. In the opening bars, for example, the accents are not sudden emphases but perhaps sighs, the *pp* dynamic full of regret and the triplet figurations troubled interjections. The songlike middle section needs a vocal rise and fall and a rich, sonorous *f* where marked. Save a little tone for the final *ppp* as the protagonist falls into a slumber.

B:2 Louise Farrenc Étude in D flat

This Étude is a real treasure, with its passionate and agitated middle section encased by a beautiful 'song without words'. Those students who have explored the delights of some of Mendelssohn's *Songs without Words* will have no problem relating to and understanding this attractive and engaging piece.

The middle section (bars 30–59) is less predictable in its harmonies and rather more demanding in its coordination between the hands and control of balance, so I would start with this. So much does the overall fluency depend on easy and fluid semiquaver movements, each finger knowing its role, that it is crucial to be fastidious and completely consistent with fingering. Bars 34–40 need particular attention. I would practise these bars slowly, without pedal – exaggerating the quietness of the RH embellishments and almost too boldly projecting the tenor melody until this is second nature – then increase the speed, gradually adding more subtlety, shape and flexibility.

The outer sections similarly rely on excellent balance to convey the song-like character, but this time within the RH. A strongly delineated balance is essential and will also help to prevent the harmonies becoming too blurred and the texture obfuscated once pedal is added. One possible approach is to use slightly flatter, relaxed fingers on the semiquavers and a more direct end-of-finger approach for the melodic notes, keeping the weight to the outside of the hand. A finger-held legato line at the top, and holding the pedal at the point of damper lift, will allow more time for gentle pedal changes on the quickly changing harmonies.

Musically, the piece will come to life with expressive rubato, dynamic rise and fall, and some judicious and warm pedalling, strongly suggested by the idiom and the *molto legato* marking. Considering words or a narrative will help to inspire ideas as to the pacing and direction of the melody; your student could visit the solo melodic line on its own to consider just how it should sound, independent of the accompaniment. Allow the middle section to gather its own momentum: don't force a tempo change but find a way to engage with the change of mood. Above all, your student should enjoy and embrace this Étude as if it were a piece of poetry, taking the listener with them on their personal musical journey.

B:3 P. I. Tchaikovsky Juin: Barcarolle

Tchaikovsky is renowned for his melodies and characterful fantasy, and 'June' is no exception, with its addictive opening tune. Perhaps explore with your student the slow movement of the First Piano Concerto, with its slow, barcarolle opening and contrasting sections reminiscent of incidental music.

The technical challenges lie primarily in developing a good physical memory, exquisite balance and warm but subtle pedal. Consider first bars 83–6 (repeated later an octave lower) and bars 48–51, working at both sections as consecutive chords, without pedal, until the hands can feel their way confidently down the sequence. The balance between melody and accompaniment is particularly challenging on the quaver E♭ on the last beat of bar 8; this note, and similar ones, must be independently projected over the lower notes and not get engulfed – not easy to do on a fourth finger.

The pedal needs to support the bass of the harmonies. In bar 3, the bottom G should sound through until the A and then the A to the B♭, the pedal changing with the harmony after the bass note has sounded but before it is released by the finger. From bar 32, change the pedal on the LH 5th just before the change of harmony to keep the drone-like character continuous; and in the second G major section (from bar 40), students could use pedal to highlight the phrasing and throw the emphasis onto the second beat.

'June' has numerous changes of mood, from the melancholy of the opening song to the folk-like second section (from bar 32) and celebratory, dance-influenced third (from bar 40). Students should allow the initial melody to float in without an accent, giving it beautiful expressive dynamic shaping and an expressive rubato. Counting the pulse musically out loud while playing can really help to keep the rubato in context. Perhaps keep the first G major section quiet and slightly hazy, a distant folk band on a summer's day, and then give the dance-like section lots of energy – short, sprung chords from the key bed followed by a very dramatic but warm-toned ff – with a long, exhausted pause before the stars mentioned in the epigram shine once again.

C:1 Isaac Albéniz Rumores de La Caleta (Murmurs from La Caleta)

One of the piano's qualities is its ability to conjure up the sound of different instruments and voices. Hot Mediterranean sunshine seems to emanate from every bar of this piece, in which flamenco-like figurations, proud and confident in their crisp rhythms, alternate with more soulful, songlike outpourings in which the tonality and melodic inflection seem to evoke the centuries-old culture of Moorish Spain. Imagining a Goya painting such as *The Parasol*, warm and intense in colour, might help your student to engage fully with this vivid, impassioned style.

Well curved, responsive fingers are needed to produce incisive articulation at the outset. Close contact with the keys is needed for crisp control and attack in the staccato bars, while lifting the fingers cleanly will give a guitar-like definition to the scale figures. Feeling to the base of the key, using the pads of the fingers while applying arm weight to support them, will help students to develop depth of tone for the RH *cantando* lines at bar 26. A good starting point for understanding the central section at bar 75 might be to establish the relative importance of melody, bass line and semiquaver syncopations; practising the inner chords silently while projecting the melodic line will help your student to distinguish between melody and accompaniment in the same hand.

Managing the frequent changes of speed convincingly is one of the main challenges in performance. A one-in-a-bar feel, with clearly defined rhythms, gives energy to the opening section, while the more relaxed pace seems to suit the languorous harmonies and quasi-improvised melodic lines of the *Meno mosso* sections. Frequent hairpins add shape to the LH figures from bar 7, with the pedal, lifted cleanly as marked, highlighting contrasts in articulation. The spirit of improvisation is most evident in the guitar-like flourishes and cadenzas during which time seems suspended, and the opportunity to linger at the *rits.* that punctuate the 'vocal' lines of the central F major section should not be missed.

C:2 Claude Debussy Arabesque No. 2   (TB)

The term 'arabesque', often applied to a style of decoration in architecture, is used here to describe a light-hearted style of piano writing, charming and youthful in its energy. This second of Debussy's *Deux arabesques* fits broadly into three main sections, with sprightly, rhythmic music surrounding a more expansive mood midway. Although it is an early work, already there are hints of the textural ideas developed in the composer's later works, especially in the pedalled sonorities of the *meno mosso*.

Light, nimble fingerwork assisted by a flexible wrist will give definition to the RH's opening triplet figures. Greater impetus will add brilliance to louder moments, however, while accented chords are best served by some arm weight. Slightly leaning the upper body towards the direction of travel will assist bigger movements on the keyboard (e.g. in bars 23–6), and leaps can be achieved by a lateral movement of the hand and forearm. In bars 37–61, your student will need to employ a variety of touches to convey the mixture of staccato, legato and short slurs, which occur at times in combination. The pedal will play a key role in creating sonority in the *meno mosso* at bar 82; elsewhere, however, any pedalling decisions need to be balanced against the need for textural clarity.

To help them manage the delicate opening bars – perhaps the most challenging area of the piece – it may be wise for your student to check the piano's responsiveness at the start of their exam. A wide dynamic range, from **ppp** to *più f*, is employed throughout, with frequent hairpins serving to underline musical contours. Clearly defined and sprightly rhythms, with accurate spacing of quaver triplets and rests, give way to a more spacious feel at bar 37. The shift from E major to E flat major at bar 56 is worthy of savouring, while the unexpected move to F major in bar 86 seems to heighten the dreamlike atmosphere of the *meno mosso*.

C:3 J. P. Johnson Over the Bars (TB)

Any student who enjoys a pianistic workout will be attracted to the ragtime-inspired rhythms and athletic stride bass figures in this piece. Contrasts of texture characterise each of the four main sections, while the melodic inventiveness and energy are guaranteed to bring a smile to any player's face. A large hand span is an asset for managing the wide stretches and chords, and some busier sections may benefit from being memorised. Slightly tempering the suggested metronome mark to perhaps ♩ = 152 may ease some of the demands without adversely affecting the musical outcome.

Fluency and accuracy in the LH jumps will be dependent on a confident lateral swing of the arm and a sure eye. Initially adding an extra octave to the single bass notes at bar 9 will make the printed distance seem easier, while spatial awareness can be developed by practising slowly without looking at the keyboard. Changes in position in the melody need to be anticipated, using the arm to direct the hand swiftly towards each new position. Lateral freedom will facilitate the slurred figures at bar 41, using the suggested combination of fingers 5/3 and 4/2 to aid legato. Learning the second-inversion chords in bars 65–8 from memory from the outset, feeling all four notes under the fingers, might be the best approach as they descend chromatically.

The sparseness of dynamic indications provides a clean palette for exploring contrasts between sections: a gentle start, for example, would throw into relief the more extrovert rhythmic energy and changes of register as the tonality shifts to F major. The slurred figures at bar 41 perhaps suggest a lighter, more airy approach, which in turn enables full impact to the repeat at bar 69, in which the LH octaves dominate the texture. Although short dabs of pedal may help to sustain the 10ths and widely spaced chords, especially if they need to be arpeggiated, drier, unpedalled textures lend overall clarity to the detail and swift harmonic changes.